EFFECTIVE POLICE SUPERVISION STUDY GUIDE

Good police officers are often promoted to supervisory positions with little or none of the training it takes to be a good manager. An understanding of group behaviors and organizational dynamics is necessary to grasp the fundamentals of managing police officers. The *Effective Police Supervision Study Guide* coordinates with the core text used in many college-level classes and police departments to teach supervisory practices in criminal justice. This study guide prepares both students and professionals for academic or promotional exams, offering them an opportunity to fully review the material so that they are well-prepared for testing.

This new edition, like the new edition of the textbook it accompanies, includes information on the following topics: police accountability, police involvement with news media, the challenges of dealing with social media, updates on legal considerations, and ways to respond to current issues facing law enforcement with COVID-19 and managing protests.

Chris Rush Burkey is an Assistant Professor in the Criminal Justice and Criminology Department at East Tennessee State University. She received her B.A. and M.A. in Criminal Justice and Criminology from East Tennessee State University and Ph.D. in Criminal Justice from the University of Arkansas at Little Rock. She has published books and book chapters, as well as articles in peer-reviewed journals, including *Deviant Behavior* and *Violence & Gender*, and has worked with agencies handling program evaluation, prisoner re-entry, forensic training, and investigative policies and regulations.

Larry S. Miller is a Professor in the Department of Criminal Justice and Criminology at East Tennessee State University. A former law enforcement officer and crime laboratory director, Miller has authored or co-authored seven textbooks, including *Police Photography*, *Crime Scene Investigation*, *Report Writing for Criminal Justice Professionals*, and *Effective Police Supervision*. His research interests and journal publications are in the areas of policing and forensic science.

Michael C. Braswell is a Professor Emeritus at East Tennessee State University. He began his career as a prison psychologist and earned his Doctorate in Counseling Psychology from the University of Southern Mississippi in 1975. He joined the Department of Criminal Justice and Criminology at ETSU in 1977, where he taught classes on Ethics and Justice, Human Relations and Criminal Justice, and Film Studies in Crime and Justice. He is widely published, and his textbook *Justice, Crime, and Ethics* is particularly influential in the field of criminal justice.

EFFECTIVE POLICE SUPERVISION STUDY GUIDE

NINTH EDITION

CHRIS RUSH BURKEY
LARRY S. MILLER
MICHAEL C. BRASWELL

Ninth edition published 2021
by Routledge
52 Vanderbilt Avenue, New York, NY 10017

and by Routledge
2 Park Square, Milton Park, Abingdon, Oxon, OX14 4RN

Routledge is an imprint of the Taylor & Francis Group, an informa business

© 2021 Taylor & Francis

The right of Chris Rush Burkey, Larry S. Miller & Michael C. Braswell to be identified as authors of this work has been asserted by them in accordance with sections 77 and 78 of the Copyright, Designs and Patents Act 1988.

All rights reserved. No part of this book may be reprinted or reproduced or utilised in any form or by any electronic, mechanical, or other means, now known or hereafter invented, including photocopying and recording, or in any information storage or retrieval system, without permission in writing from the publishers.

Trademark notice: Product or corporate names may be trademarks or registered trademarks, and are used only for identification and explanation without intent to infringe.

First edition published by Anderson 1990
Eighth edition published by Routledge 2017

Library of Congress Cataloging-in-Publication Data
Names: Rush Burkey, Chris author. | Miller, Larry, 1953 August
  26– author. | Braswell, Michael, author.
Title: Effective police supervision study guide / Chris Rush Burkey, Larry S.
  Miller & Michael C. Braswell.
Description: 9th edition. | New York, NY : Routledge, 2021. |
  Includes bibliographical references and index.
Identifiers: LCCN 2020042125 (print) | LCCN 2020042126 (ebook) |
ISBN 9780367260583 (hardcover) | ISBN 9780367265892 (paperback) |
ISBN 9780429294044 (ebook)
Subjects: LCSH: Police--Supervision of.
Classification: LCC HV7936.S8 M67 2021 (print) | LCC HV7936.S8 (ebook) |
  DDC 363.2/2--dc23
LC record available at https://lccn.loc.gov/2020042125
LC ebook record available at https://lccn.loc.gov/2020042126

ISBN: 978-0-367-26058-3 (hbk)
ISBN: 978-0-367-26589-2 (pbk)
ISBN: 978-0-429-29404-4 (ebk)

Typeset in Garamond, Helvetica Neue, Optima and Stone Serif
by codeMantra

CONTENTS

A Note to the Student	vii
CHAPTER 1—Supervision—The Management Task	1
CHAPTER 2—Community-Oriented Policing and Problem Solving—Improving Neighborhood Quality of Life	13
CHAPTER 3—Interpersonal Communications—Striving for Effectiveness	23
CHAPTER 4—Motivation—A Prerequisite for Success	37
CHAPTER 5—Leadership—The Integrative Variable	49
CHAPTER 6—Team Building—Maximizing the Group Process	61
CHAPTER 7—Change—Coping with Organizational Life	73
CHAPTER 8—Performance Appraisal—The Key to Police Personnel Development	81
CHAPTER 9—Training, Coaching, Counseling, and Mentoring—Helping Officers Grow and Develop	97
CHAPTER 10—Discipline—An Essential Element of Police Supervision	111
CHAPTER 11—Internal Discipline—A System of Accountability	123
CHAPTER 12—Supervising the Difficult Employee—Special Considerations	139
CHAPTER 13—Supervising Minorities—Respecting Individual and Cultural Differences	151
CHAPTER 14—Tactical Operations—Critical Incident Deployment	167

CHAPTER 15—Labor Relations—Problem Solving through Constructive Conflict   **173**

CHAPTER 16—Homeland Security and Terrorism—A Changing Role   **189**

Answer Key to Objective Questions   199

A NOTE TO THE STUDENT

This study guide was created to complement *Effective Police Supervision*, Ninth Edition, by Larry S. Miller, Henry W. More, and Michael Braswell. It is not designed to serve as a substitute for the textbook. You will need to read the book to fully understand the concepts of effective police supervision, and you will need the textbook to complete portions of this guide.

The best strategy is to look at this study guide prior to reading each chapter of the textbook. First, read the Learning Objectives and Key Terms before each chapter. These will help you focus on key material as you read the text. After reading the chapter in the text, it may be helpful to outline the chapter, and it will be useful to write out definitions and/or examples for each of the Key Terms listed. You may wish to include other terms and concepts from the text, which are not listed in the guide.

Your professor may assign particular Discussion Topics and Questions or Case Studies from the text.

Thinking about and crafting responses to the issues raised in these questions and scenarios, whether or not they are formally assigned, will help you to grasp key concepts and synthesize the material in a meaningful and applicable way that goes beyond learning by rote.

Finally, the questions and answer key provided in this guide will provide one way for you to measure how well you are grasping the material.

We hope this study guide proves helpful in your studies of police supervision. If you have comments on how the guide can be improved for future editions or if you find mistakes, you may e-mail Dr. Larry S. Miller at millerls@etsu.edu.

CHAPTER 1 Supervision—The Management Task

LEARNING OBJECTIVES

1. Identify skills needed by a first-line supervisor.
2. Define knowledge-based skills.
3. Identify human skills.
4. Compare conceptual and affective skills.
5. Describe a positive attitude toward management's expectations of the supervisor.
6. Define loyalty.
7. Characterize the subordinate's expectations of the supervisor.
8. Identify key elements of participation.
9. Describe the process of conflict resolution.
10. List the functions performed by supervisors when relating to subordinates.

KEY TERMS

- affective skills
- conceptual skills
- dynamic organization
- Hu-TACK participation
- human skills
- integrity
- knowledge-based skills
- loyalty responding to management
- management expectations of the supervisor
- officer behavior
- performance
- positive attitude
- self-appraisal
- subordinate expectations
- supervisory skill areas
- tactical skills
- transition

Chapter Summary

I Transition to First-Line Supervisor

The first-line supervisor is at the organizational focal point between line officers and other police managers. It is important to learn the positive aspects of reaching the position of first-line supervisor and also be able to understand why the first-line supervisor's position is not for everyone, by examining the negative aspects of the position. Good supervisors do not just happen; they must be cultivated. The first-line supervisor has become an important part of management who is responsible for improving the quality of work life.

Police work has become more and more complex, and it seems reasonable that problems facing today's officers will only increase the complexity of the job. The supervisor must respond with imagination and innovation. One of the most difficult new duties facing the supervisor is being an effective disciplinarian. The supervisor must learn to meet the needs of both officers and the organization, developing a wide range of skills.

II Supervisory Skills

Once an officer assumes the position of a first-line supervisor, his or her role changes drastically and tasks become managerial. It is a supervisor's responsibility to emphasize the development of subordinates' skills, rather than doing everything himself or herself. In order to maximize effectiveness, a supervisor must attain objectives through the efforts of others by becoming operationally effective in one or more of the following skill areas, known by the acronym **Hu-TACK**.

Human skills (Hu). An effective supervisor has the ability to be able to effectively listen and discuss problems with subordinates and deal with each officer as an individual. The effective supervisor also sets the standard of professionalism by example and encourages **positive attitudes** through individual encouragement and motivates the employees. This supervisor has the ability to resolve conflicts effectively.

Tactical skills (T). Tactics, used by supervisors, comes into play when it is necessary to apply leadership that enables one to control a situation and accomplish a mission in a field situation. It is a time when everything is brought into focus by providing purpose, direction, and motivation to an unusual occurrence. It is one of the few times that mission accomplishment overrides other factors and becomes an inviolable imperative.

Affective skills (A). The supervisor acts as a role model by demonstrating both **integrity** and **loyalty**. Moreover, the supervisor demonstrates the ability to integrate the organizational values and community values. An environment based on equality and fairness is set and demonstrates that this supervisor values the employees and their contribution to the organization.

Conceptual skills (C). The supervisor has the ability to analyze situations and make good decisions. Also, the supervisor is capable of integrating personal activities into the total organizational plan, so that agency goals are attained.

Knowledge-based skills (K). The supervisor has the ability to handle the administrative responsibilities and provides the technical support that each officer needs. The supervisor has knowledge of the policies and procedures and implements them effectively. The supervisor is responsible for the training and development of the officers.

The supervisor should do a **self-appraisal** to select managerial techniques that fit his or her style. It is also important to understand line officers and their potential, acknowledging individual differences and cultivating the talents of officers. This style of supervision allows the supervisor to arrive at decisions suitable for the employee and the organization. However, supervisors must be flexible in their approaches and recognize that a particular approach does not work every time.

Managerial networking involves flexibility in combining different supervisory approaches. Each officer should be integrated into the organization, and the focus on decision-making improves work life and productivity. The purpose of this networking is to foster self-help, exchange information, and share resources.

III *Management Expectations of the Supervisor*

To meet managerial expectations, the supervisor must develop the ability to identify the duties that relate to the management of people and emphasize them. The importance of a supervisor maintaining a **positive attitude** as a means of dealing with obstacles in a constructive manner cannot be stressed enough. A first-line supervisor must also maintain **loyalty** to upper management. When one accepts a supervisory position, one accepts the obligation to be part of the team. Management should expect the **performance** of its supervisors to be excellent. Tasks and responsibilities should be handled in a timely and professional manner. However, when a timetable cannot be realistically met, this must be conveyed and dealt with. **Responding to management** is vital. Management expects the first-line supervisor to maintain a high level of communication with them, especially to keep them aware of subordinates' concerns, desires, and suggestions. They also expect the supervisor to have the ability to efficiently prepare administrative paperwork, that is, budget requests, assigned investigations, and written employee evaluations.

As with subordinates, first-line supervisors must look upon management as made up of unique individuals. They need to identify their managers' strengths and weaknesses, work habits, and needs—and then respond accordingly. Supervisors need to be viewed by management as helpful colleagues and trustworthy professionals who are part of the management team.

IV Subordinate Expectations of the Supervisor

First-line supervisors have to deal with demands from both within and outside the agency. The primary reason for the supervisory position is the need for work to be accomplished effectively. Goals must be achieved for the organization to continue to exist.

Subordinates' needs must be recognized and met by the organization. When the needs are met by the job, then the job motivates the employee. This must be assessed continuously by the supervisor. The authors state that 85 percent of the employees will respond to the positive efforts of the supervisor, but that the greater amount of a supervisor's time is usually spent on the remaining 15 percent, who, for whatever reason, are "poor employees."

Authoritarian management should be discarded. The changed attitude of police officers has shown that they will give their best for a certain number of hours if they have a positive work environment. Today's officers look for a challenging job, an opportunity to make a contribution, self-expression, and free time for outside activities.

A. Participative Management. The process of opening the decision-making process up to employees to participate. The employee must be empowered in order to accomplish assigned tasks; thus, power must be shared. This participative management may reduce the number of traditional managers needed, but will increase the need for leaders. The end result is an environment in which officers want to work.

B. Conflict Resolution. The ability of the supervisor to assist subordinates with problems that are both internal and external to the department while being able to distinguish between real employee complaints and petty bickering or mere griping. Conflict identification and resolution are considered by many supervisors to be the most important function of the first-line supervisor.

V Peer Expectations of the Supervisor

Supervision is a joint effort between supervisors in order to accomplish the tasks and goals of the organization successfully. Reciprocal, positive relationships between peers require communication and consideration. The first-line supervisor must learn the importance and effectiveness of "end-of-shift" communication between supervisors. They must also learn the value of conferences or staff meetings and utilize them as a means to provide adequate time for discussion of matters that require a complete understanding of the organization's position on procedures and policies. Successful worker relationships focus on the work rather than personalities. The ability to get along with people is the hallmark of the professional. Supervisors should deal with any inevitable criticisms in a constructive manner.

Multiple-Choice Questions (Circle the Best Answer)

1. According to More and Miller, first-line supervisors are:

    a. a nonintegral part of management.

    b. indirectly responsible for improving the quality of work life.

    c. an integral part of management.

    d. a necessary evil.

2. _____ is what most first-line supervisors deal with in the workplace. The greater the supervisor's knowledge in this area, the greater the prospect that both individual and organizational goals will be attained.

    a. Paperwork

    b. Scheduling

    c. Task selection

    d. Human behavior

3. If supervisors are successful in the performance of their duties,

    a. they will be promoted quickly.

    b. the organization will become more effective.

    c. they will play a minor role in responding to change that impacts the organization.

    d. they will receive additional training within one year after being promoted.

4. Transition from a line position to a first-line supervisor means that, administratively, supervisors

    a. should distance themselves from officers.

    b. should not be involved in the decision-making process.

    c. must not become a part of management.

    d. usually head a given operation and become part of management.

5. Conversion to the position of first-line supervisor

    a. presents little challenge.

    b. demands the ability to accept and adapt to change.

    c. should be accomplished with very little effort.

    d. may never be attained if the ecology of the organization is known.

6. Affective skills deal with

    a. emotions, agency goals, values.

    b. attitudes, interpretation, analysis.

    c. analysis, interpretation, resolution.

    d. emotions, values, attitudes.

7. Knowledge-based skills deal with

    a. emotions, agency goals, values.

    b. attitudes, interpretation, analysis.

    c. analysis, interpretation, resolution.

    d. emotions, values, attitudes.

8. Supervisors demonstrating knowledge-based skills will

    a. provide officers with appropriate administrative and technical support.

    b. possibly consider each officer's workload, but not as a priority.

    c. show an interest in seeing that their officers carry out assignments if time permits.

    d. implement departmental policy and procedures at all costs.

9. In order for supervisors to accomplish work through people, they must

    a. know the abilities and limitations of each employee.

    b. apply different standards for each employee.

    c. set standards higher than capabilities to build in challenges for employees.

    d. all of the above.

10. Supervisors demonstrating human skills should

    a. not discuss problems with subordinates.

    b. perform as professionals and set the standards for employees.

c. order the officers to get counseling when problems arise.

d. encourage peer pressure as a means of motivation.

11. The first-line supervisor is in the best position to _____ conflicts between specialized police units by using conceptualization techniques.

    a. identify and assess

    b. assess and discipline

    c. discipline and resolve

    d. identify and resolve

12. When a new policy or general order is promulgated, the best way to react is to

    a. distribute the written policy to subordinates and refrain from any discussion.

    b. distribute the written policy and point out the weaknesses in the policy, so that the subordinates know the problems with implementation.

    c. distribute the policy and any positive or negative research that you have received on the change, so that the subordinates recognize that you are knowledgeable about the new policy.

    d. be honest with your subordinates and tell them when the policy is a poor one, so that they will respect you.

    e. be positive, distribute the policy, and respond based on a critical evaluation of ways, which will ensure that the policy is workable.

13. First-line supervisors are at the fulcrum point between management and line operations, and, therefore, must

    a. identify problem employees to upper management immediately.

    b. accomplish the tasks of interpreting rules, regulations, and policies.

    c. insulate themselves from undue influence from above and below.

    d. find out about problems with subordinates first, so that discipline can be given and the supervisor will look favorable to upper management.

14. A failure by a subordinate to perform at acceptable levels must be

    a. confronted and resolved in favor of the organization.

    b. reviewed by the supervisor and then standards re-evaluated to fit the individual needs of the employee.

c. resolved with discipline to set an example for the rest.

d. ignored and the employee watched for improvement over time.

15. In order for officers to feel a part of the organization,
    a. they should be allowed to achieve individual needs even if agency needs are put on hold.
    b. satisfying organizational goals must be their focus.
    c. they should be included in the decision-making process across the board.
    d. job satisfaction should be accomplished by allowing officers to achieve individual needs while organizational needs are satisfied.

16. Progressive police agencies open the decision-making process to
    a. all employees.
    b. employees who are loyal to the administrators.
    c. employees who have first-hand knowledge and are allowed to study problems confronting the agency.
    d. first-line supervisors and above in rank structure.

17. The real byproduct of participative management is that it
    a. shifts the burden off top administrators.
    b. creates a work environment in which officers want to work.
    c. requires more supervisors to get the job done.
    d. requires an overhaul of human nature.

18. Successful accomplishment of tasks and goal attainment requires
    a. no consideration given as to how the supervisor's actions affect the duties of others.
    b. coordination and cooperation between supervisors.
    c. a strict code of order giving and follow-up.
    d. that the supervisor report only to the chief to avoid miscommunication.

19. Successful dealings with peers require

    a. management by discipline.

    b. information hoarding.

    c. independent problem solving.

    d. joint resolution of problems.

20. The authors stress that a positive method for discussion before implementation of a new policy is the

    a. end-of-shift briefing.

    b. beginning-of-shift briefing.

    c. conference setting.

    d. memorandum of understanding.

True or False Questions

1. It is necessary for a supervisor to consider both the social needs of the officers and the tasks to be performed.

2. According to the Bureau of Justice report, 55 percent of those who were threatened with the use of force by police believed it was excessive.

3. Good supervision is the result of the serious application of one's knowledge about human behavior to the work situation.

4. A first-line supervisor must become personally acquainted with each employee and treat them as individuals.

5. According to More and Miller, middle and top management want to believe that rules are supported by first-line supervision.

6. Supervisors should be able to stereotype the manager in order to better understand that manager's management methods.

7. An effective first-line supervisor will identify his or her own style of management and stick with it no matter what the individual situation presents in order to show consistency.

8. First-line supervisors should project an air of caring by being constantly available for help and guidance and by accepting and resolving problems as they occur, while exhibiting a genuine desire to trust each employee.

9. First-line supervisors must learn that employee complaints are just gripe sessions for the employee and require no supervisory action.

10. According to More and Miller, the supervisor's position is one of conflict identification and resolution.

11. Focusing on the work to be done, rather than the personalities of those involved results in positive relationships with peers.

12. A supervisor's success depends on the qualities and qualifications brought to the managerial process and the method used in resolving the conflict.

13. The ability to get along with people is the hallmark of the professional and a sign of maturity.

14. Individuals who think positively are result-oriented and deal with obstacles in a constructive manner.

15. According to More and Miller, middle and top management expectations of the first-line supervisor include a positive attitude, accomplishment of tasks, and responding to requests from upper management, but there is little concern about loyalty to the department.

CHAPTER 2 Community-Oriented Policing and Problem Solving—Improving Neighborhood Quality of Life

LEARNING OBJECTIVES

1. Define community policing.
2. Describe the importance of empowerment.
3. List the responsibilities of a first-line supervisor in community policing.
4. Describe how a supervisor should build partnerships within the department.
5. Define collaboration.
6. List eight different potential resources for problem solving.
7. Identify some of the elements of quality supervision.
8. Define process facilitation.
9. Describe the typical day of a community policing supervisor.
10. List and define the four components of problem solving.
11. List several reasons why one should manage failure.

KEY TERMS

- actors
- analysis
- assessment
- collaboration partnerships
- community enhancement
- empowerment
- environmental surveys
- incidents
- institutional
- managing failure
- offenders
- problem solving
- process facilitation third parties
- quality supervision victims
- response
- risk taking
- scanning
- sequence of events
- supervisory techniques

Chapter Summary

I Community Policing—What Is It?

Community policing is a philosophy of policing where officers work and build close relationships with community residents. This is accomplished when officers create informal contacts with residents and institutions serving the area. Community policing allows law enforcement officials to not only address crimes, but also explore and understand the causes of crime within the community.

Along with identifying problems, the department can focus on community resources to solve the problems. To be successful, top management must express the values and mission of community policing to all levels within the organization.

II Empowerment

Empowerment of line personnel and first-line supervisors is an essential component of community policing. The five identified characteristics of officers and supervisors operating in a community policing organization are as follows:

1. Risk taking.
2. Originality.
3. Creativity.
4. Individuality.
5. Problem solving.

A. **Empowerment.** The conscious decision of the chief executive officer to allow others to assume decision-making through delegated power and authority. The supervisor's role requires that he or she coach, support, and help officers in planning, analyzing, and solving community problems.

B. **Quality Supervision.** Involves shared decision-making, teamwork, creativity, and innovation.

III Process Facilitation

The first-line supervisor is responsible for conveying the importance of community policing to the police officers. The officers need to be shown that the involvement in the community and problem solving are real work.

A. **Process Facilitator.** A supervisor who communicates openly becomes a team member and encourages officers to participate actively in problem solving.

When the first-line supervisor accomplishes becoming a process facilitator, he or she can effectively serve as a conduit to relay information up the chain of command. It is imperative to the success of the community policing program to build **partnerships** within the agency. Through these partnerships come resources to solve the problems as they become identified. The first-line supervisor must "sell" the problems to all units and foster a relationship that assures commitment to the cause.

IV *Collaboration*

For community policing to work, a wide range of resources must be used to solve problems. Identification of resources and the development of collaborative efforts are essential. Line officers should have a means for requesting services (Figure 2.4). Supervisors should monitor and evaluate the collaboration process. Liaison and follow-up are essential to the success of collaboration.

V *Problem Solving*

The modern approach to problem solving is a positive orientation that is proactive in nature. Thus, problems are viewed from the perspective of the entire community. Citizens, police departments, and other agencies unite to work proactively in identifying community problems and in correcting them. Within the police department, detectives and line officers use the problem-solving approach to identify, analyze, and respond to factors that often lead to citizen complaints or requests for help.

The four components of problem solving are as follows:

1. *Scanning*—identifies the problems and prioritizes them. The scanning phase also involves the assignment of personnel.

2. *Analysis*—learning what the problem's causes and effects are. Analysis involves the collection of all available information (including **actors** and **incidents**).

3. *Response*—initiating actions to either correct or alleviate the problem. May involve engaging the resources of other community agencies or resources.

4. *Assessment*—process of determining the effectiveness of the response. May involve administration of a community survey to gather information on attitudes and opinions toward the police response.

VI *Supervising the Community Policing Officers*

The authoritative style of supervision is not conducive to managing a community policing officer—officers must be given greater control over their work environment. A few rewards to community policing officers are as follows:

1. They have greater control over the work performed.

2. They have increased responsibility for the work performed and increased autonomy.

3. They have direct involvement in the decision-making process due to increased participation in problem solving.

Therefore, it appears that community policing officers can obtain greater job satisfaction. The first-line supervisor becomes more of a resource person and manager for the officers. First-line supervisors must spend time with the officers in the neighborhood if they are to be able to help the officers with the community problems they face.

VII *Managing Failure*

Managing in a community policing environment must be done in an informal manner. This is because this problem-solving approach is a new technique for officers, and the supervisors must accept that they will make mistakes and failures will occur. It is the supervisor's responsibility to manage and control those failures, so that positive results can ultimately occur. Documenting failures is also important, so that this information can be shared with other interested people. This will allow the agency to identify areas that need training. A teamwork philosophy must prevail if community policing is to be successful.

A. **Managing Failure.** This is a process of depersonalizing failure and judging the actual event and not the involved individual.

   Realizing that failure should lead to growth and not negative discipline for the officer is important for the supervisor.

Multiple-Choice Questions (Circle the Best Answer)

1. All but which of the following is true in relation to community policing?

    a. It grabs headlines throughout the nation.

    b. There is a consensus in defining it.

c. Police conferences discuss it in depth.

d. Special training can prepare officers to carry out problem-solving programs.

2. Community policing is a transitional process in which the _____ removes barriers that impede change.

   a. sergeant

   b. beat cop

   c. chief executive officer

   d. citizen

3. All but which of the following is true about the working definition of community policing?

   a. Officers work jointly with community residents.

   b. Consideration is given to the needs of the community.

   c. The police work to solve a community's problems for them.

   d. The causes of crime are agreed upon.

4. An essential ingredient of community policing is

   a. empowerment of officers and first-line supervisors.

   b. involvement of upper management.

   c. increased funding.

   d. flexibility of shift assignments.

5. With the introduction of community policing, the _____ is/are at center stage.

   a. chief executive officer

   b. residents and business owners

   c. community policing officers

   d. first-line supervisors

6. Quality supervisors must personify the attributes of _____ if community policing is to succeed.

   a. a communicator and an authoritarian

   b. an authoritarian and a role model

   c. a facilitator and a coach

   d. a coach and an authoritarian

7. During the facilitation process, the supervisor must do all of the following except

   a. take over the task of an independent problem solver.

   b. convince police officers that community engagement and problem solving are real police work.

   c. genuinely support organizational changes.

   d. articulate and reinforce the philosophy of community policing.

8. Responsibilities of a first-line supervisor for supervising community policing officers include

   a. personalizing failures and judging the individual officer to decide whether the officer is fit for the program.

   b. encouraging officers not to take risks, but to discuss problems with the supervisor first before acting.

   c. ensuring the retention of beat integrity when problem solving.

   d. discouraging inventiveness when problem solving.

9. Supervisors can reinforce the collaboration process of problem solving by

   a. requiring detailed paperwork.

   b. checking the efforts of officers.

   c. requiring notification of every effort.

   d. using a "hands-off" approach that encourages independence.

10. Failure should lead to

    a. a review board.

    b. growth.

c. punishment.

d. reparation.

11. All but which of the following describes the first-line supervisor's functions under empowerment?

    a. Mentor.

    b. Manipulator.

    c. Motivator.

    d. Facilitator.

12. The first phase of the problem-solving approach is

    a. searching.

    b. seeking.

    c. scanning.

    d. scope.

True or False Questions

1. Philosophically, community policing is an insignificant change in the provision of police services.

2. Community policing gives officers an opportunity to move closer to the community.

3. Community policing is a transitional process in which the chief executive officer removes barriers that impede change.

4. Community policing, to be successful, demands radical changes over time if there is to be significant alteration in the way the organization attains goals.

5. Line officers and supervisors are the recipients of a minor shift of power and authority.

6. Empowerment is when the supervisor encourages officers to "stay out of trouble" or "not bother" their sergeant.

7. When empowerment occurs, community policing is doomed.

8. Supervisors must convey to all officers the importance of community policing and that it is real police work.

9. Under community policing, isolation between officers and detectives must always be reduced.

10. The chief executive officer is the key to community policing, and all other units should support the problem-solving efforts.

11. Methods in which first-line supervisors monitor and respond to citizen complaints affect the credibility of the line officers as well as the police department.

12. Community policing involves giving officers greater control over their working conditions.

13. The first-line supervisor must manage in a formal manner to avoid mistakes.

14. When managing failure, a first-line supervisor must personalize the failure of the community policing officer and evaluate the individual officer to decide if he or she is fit to belong to the unit.

15. The importance of collaboration in community policing is that it can provide a variety of resources to resolve identifiable problems.

16. The analysis component of the problem-solving approach involves identification of a community problem.

17. The problem-solving approach may assess the effectiveness of community policing through public surveys.

CHAPTER 3 Interpersonal Communications—Striving for Effectiveness

LEARNING OBJECTIVES

1. List the reasons why a first-line supervisor should become a skillful communicator.
2. Identify, in order of importance, the tasks performed by a supervisor.
3. Define interpersonal communication.
4. Describe elements of the realistic communication process.
5. Compare one-way and two-way communications.
6. Identify the major barriers to the communication process.
7. Describe how to overcome communication barriers.
8. Identify the ways a supervisor can provide positive feedback.
9. Describe the techniques a supervisor can use to improve listening skills.
10. Identify the key characteristics of body language.
11. Describe the importance of paralanguage and facial expressions when communicating.
12. Discuss how diversity training may benefit officers.
13. List things an officer can do when communicating with someone who is hearing-impaired.

KEY TERMS

- art of listening
- barriers
- communication patterns
- communication process
- communication tasks
- decoding
- encoding
- facial expression
- importance of communications
- intercultural communications
- interpreters
- limited English proficiency
- lip-reading
- name reference library
- nonverbal communications
- one-way communication
- physiological barriers
- proxemics
- psychological barriers
- realistic communications process
- semantics
- sign language

Chapter Summary

I Importance of Communication Skills

The ability to communicate effectively is a requisite to being a successful supervisor. As tasks performed by the first-line supervisor become more complex, it is imperative that a supervisor develop excellent communication skills. Interpersonal communication exists at all levels of management. However, the first-line supervisor interacts continually with officers at the operational level. The first-line supervisor is the primary communication point between upper management and the line officer.

Of 53 representative tasks a first-line supervisor completes, 51 percent involve communication. The effectiveness of communication is dependent on the communicator's awareness of communication needs and the ability to express an idea clearly and influence another person.

II Communication Process

Communication is the exchange of information between people. Effective communication involves transmission of a message, **decoding** the message, and the recipient correctly interpreting and understanding the message. This communication process is exceedingly complex when you factor attitudes, skills, knowledge, opinions, and other pre-existing factors. **Gatekeeping** refers to the sender determining the relevance and importance of information. Because of operational autonomy, the first-line supervisor is in a position to control the amount and nature of information entering the system.

Elements of a **realistic communication process** include sender, **encoding**, channel, decoding, receiver, noise, and **feedback** (Figure 3.4). Content and context are also important considerations in effective communication.

There can be **one-way communication**, as an order to act, or **two-way communication**, in which there is an exchange.

A. **One-Way Communication.** The communicator sends out a message. Traditionally, this has dominated police supervisory techniques with subordinates.

One-way communication is preferred when speed and compliance are imperative and orderliness is significant. It protects the sender's authority and power because errors are never acknowledged. This is used frequently in Special Weapons and Tactics (SWAT) team environments.

B. **Two-Way Communication.** Two-way communication occurs when the receiver provides feedback to the sender. Two-way communication improves accuracy of the message and provides a greater understanding.

However, with two-way communication, the sender must share the power and authority.

III Barriers to Communication

There are always **barriers** to communication, which can be either physical or psychological. Barriers generally involve concern about one's knowledge of the subject, the possibility of being looked upon with displeasure, jeopardizing one's status, environmental influences, personal expectations, and **semantics**. Because subordinates are careful not to affect their personal position with the supervisor, barriers are formed, which impede open two-way communication.

IV Overcoming Barriers to Communication

Supervisors must recognize that barriers do exist. They need to attempt to develop a supportive relationship with subordinates if they are going to be able to evaluate the situations that arise. Real two-way communication exists when subordinates accept a supervisor as someone who helps and supports, rather than one who forces, demands, or orders.

V Feedback

A. Feedback. Information received by the sender from the recipient, so that the sender may modify and correct the initial message. Feedback is most useful when used as a way to help the recipient understand communication.

Feedback works best in an environment based on developed relationships and trust. For feedback to be most effective, it should be selective, specific, descriptive, issue oriented, and based on facts, rather than personality. Because even constructive criticism is difficult to face, supervisors should provide feedback at an appropriate time and place. The ultimate goal is improved communication and performance. Furthermore, feedback should also contribute to an individual's knowledge about their performance.

VI The Art of Listening

The effective supervisor has the responsibility to develop the skill of listening. Listening is an active process. A good listener makes every attempt to get the message. When a supervisor listens to a subordinate, that employee must be made to feel that no one will be allowed to interrupt their conversation. Listeners must always keep an open mind and recognize their own biases. They must not let their personal feelings prevent communication. If the supervisor as a listener addresses situations intellectually, it allows officers' ideas to be heard. Listeners must look for implications to get clues about what is really being said. This requires the listener to stop talking and hear what is being said.

VII Nonverbal Communication

Nonverbal communication includes the stance, gestures, **facial expressions**, and other nonverbal cues used when delivering a message. It is used primarily to convey emotions, desires, and preferences. The face is the main communicator of emotions.

Eye contact can be used very effectively to control communication. It reinforces talking with an employee because it demonstrates that the employee has the supervisor's undivided attention. A supervisor who can use nonverbal communication effectively can use cues to support and reinforce communication, which will reduce the possibility of the receiver misinterpreting the sender's message.

Nonverbal communication can also be conveyed through **paralanguage**, which is voice volume, tone, pitch, and/or inflection.

VIII Communicating with Non-English-Speaking Individuals

When attempting to communicate with a non-English-speaking individual, an officer should try to procure a translator. The translator may be a family member, neighbor, fellow officer, or other agency member.

IX Intercultural Communications

Becoming educated in **intercultural communications** improves communication between police officers and individuals of different cultural backgrounds. Such training allows officers to be sensitive to the etiquette and traditions and communication styles of other cultures.

X Hearing-Impaired Individuals

It is estimated that 21 million people in the United States have a **hearing impairment**. Individuals with a hearing impairment can be identified through careful observation of the person. Once the impairment is identified, the communicating officer should face the person directly, get the person's attention, speak slowly, and avoid overemphasizing his or her lip movement. An **interpreter** can facilitate communication between hearing and deaf persons.

When a hearing-impaired person is arrested, he or she should be provided with an interpreter and advised of constitutional rights with a printed form of the Miranda warning.

Multiple-Choice Questions (Circle the Best Answer)

1. A breakdown in communication is an inevitable consequence of

    a. the natural tendency to be easily distracted.

    b. the inability to properly interpret what is said.

    c. the increasing problem of the short attention span.

    d. none of the above.

2. Interpersonal communication exists at every level of any organization, but is most prevalent at the

    a. mid-management level.

    b. operational level.

    c. upper-management level.

    d. all of the above.

3. According to More and Miller, at the very least, communication is the "lifeblood" of the organization because

    a. it is the process that ties the whole organization together.

    b. everyone must talk the same language in order to communicate.

    c. it is a resource in constant use and abuse.

    d. you cannot avoid it.

4. In order for communication to be effective, it must be

    a. reinforced through repetition.

    b. nurtured by all levels of management from the top down.

    c. inherent.

    d. approached cautiously.

5. One study of first-line supervisors cited in the text showed that they spend the least amount of their communication time communicating with

   a. other supervisors.
   b. citizens.
   c. superiors.
   d. subordinates.

6. A successful communicator is the one who

   a. is not concerned about personal self-esteem.
   b. looks for someone to blame.
   c. upon realization that he or she has not explained something adequately will still expect the officer to understand and do the job correctly.
   d. does not have a lot to say because others always understand him or her.

7. The sender of the information determines the relevance and the importance of the information, which is known as

   a. operational autonomy.
   b. gatekeeping.
   c. channeling.
   d. censoring.

8. Because of _____, the first-line supervisor is in the position of controlling the amount and the nature of information that enters the information system.

   a. gatekeeping
   b. operational autonomy
   c. channeling
   d. censoring

9. The first-line supervisor must be concerned about the _____, as it can prove to be more meaningful than the _____.

   a. context, content
   b. content, context

c. verbal message, nonverbal message

d. nonverbal message, verbal message

10. According to More and Miller, first-line supervisors spend _____ percent of their communication time communicating with the officers they supervise.

    a. 40

    b. 55

    c. 60

    d. 72

11. When the sender communicates without expecting or receiving feedback from the recipient, he or she is demonstrating

    a. channeling.

    b. one-way communication.

    c. two-way communication.

    d. none of the above.

12. One-way communication is preferable when

    a. feedback is required immediately.

    b. orderliness is insignificant.

    c. compliance is imperative.

    d. all of the above.

13. Two-way communication requires less planning due to

    a. the opportunity for feedback and the ability to clarify the issues.

    b. the error rate for decoding.

    c. more planning due to so many variables.

    d. the need for less understanding.

14. Advantages of two-way communication may include

    a. improved accuracy and greater understanding.

    b. no sharing of authority and responsibility.

c. less acknowledgment of the importance of communicating.

d. no recognition of the fact that subordinates need to know what is expected.

15. Supervisors who use jargon

    a. may communicate that officers may treat the people they "label" differently and not in accordance with their constitutional rights.

    b. may cloud communication.

    c. may exclude some officers from discussion.

    d. all of the above.

16. There are a number of ways of overcoming communication barriers, including all but which of the following?

    a. Use of one-way communication to reduce the "noise" created by discussion.

    b. Continual use of face-to-face communication.

    c. Repetition of communication as needed.

    d. Constant use of direct and simple language.

17. The foundation for real two-way communication occurs when subordinates accept a supervisor as someone who

    a. supports and assists.

    b. forces, demands, and orders.

    c. has a job to do that requires orders and demands to be met.

    d. has a job to do and cannot be their friend.

18. In a real working relationship, where there is true commitment from subordinates, there will be

    a. no sharing of power.

    b. mutual respect, but no genuine acceptance of one another.

    c. feelings of trust, but not mutual respect.

    d. genuine acceptance of each other.

19. A supervisor should view each officer as a member of a team by

    a. making personality judgments.

    b. stressing strengths.

    c. focusing on weaknesses.

    d. the way the officer relates items of interest about other officers.

20. A supervisor must convey to each employee that

    a. he or she makes decisions based on upper-management instructions.

    b. there is no room for flexibility in decisions based on employees' opinions.

    c. he or she is willing to accept a certain degree of risk because the positive results usually exceed the errors that will occur.

    d. a work environment where subordinates follow without questioning is of primary importance.

21. Spoken communication, in contrast to written communication,

    a. reinforces supportive relationships.

    b. creates an atmosphere characterized by a lack of trust and confidence.

    c. is less reliable due to the greater chance of misinterpretation and should be avoided.

    d. is not recommended.

22. When feedback is provided, it should be

    a. descriptive and judgmental.

    b. instructive or corrective.

    c. given immediately, regardless of circumstances to have impact.

    d. selective, but not limited to the issue at hand.

23. According to Albert Mehrabian, the three components of a message that contribute to the communication process in terms of impact are

    a. 7 percent actual words, 38 percent the way it is said, 55 percent nonverbal.

b. 40 percent actual words, 10 percent the way it is said, 50 percent nonverbal.

c. 32 percent actual words, 38 percent the way it is said, 30 percent nonverbal.

24. Body language includes
    a. posture, words, facial expressions, eye contact, body tension.
    b. posture, facial expressions, eye contact.
    c. body tension, positioning, attention.
    d. eye contact, facial expressions, words.

25. Nonverbal communication is used primarily to convey
    a. emotions.
    b. desires.
    c. preferences.
    d. all of the above.

26. Paralanguage refers to
    a. tactile communication.
    b. psychic communication.
    c. communication through voice inflections.
    d. written communication.

27. Effective eye contact can be used to
    a. display aloofness and initiate feedback.
    b. show a lack of confidence, anxiety, and aloofness.
    c. reinforce feedback, solicit or suppress the transmission of a message, and support communication.

True or False Questions

1. The need for good communication skills has become increasingly important, as the tasks performed have become easier to accomplish.

2. Effective communication means getting the meaning across; therefore, a good communicator goes into great detail, so there is a lengthy explanation.

3. Effective communication involves the transmission of the message and the recipient interpreting the message correctly.

4. When goals are compatible, there is a greater possibility that a message will be interpreted accurately.

5. The recipient of information reacts to a message based on experiences, knowledge, viewpoints, and frame of reference.

6. Barriers to communication can include concern about one's knowledge of the subject as well as the probability of being looked upon with displeasure.

7. A supervisor can obtain sound feedback only when there is reason for officers to dispel fears and concerns that impede or impair two-way communication.

8. A supportive relationship is the one in which the subordinate is allowed to influence the supervisor.

9. Listening is an active process that includes one's intellectual capacities of comprehension and evaluation.

10. Successful listeners should strive to keep an open mind and be fully cognizant of their own biases and preconceptions.

11. As a good listener, a supervisor must respond intellectually, rather than emotionally.

12. A good listener waits until the sender completes a message before responding, suspending judgment, which is polite, but has little or no effect on misinterpretation.

13. A supervisor can improve learning effectiveness by giving undivided attention to the speaker, attempting to listen emotionally, and adjusting to the sender's message.

14. An effective supervisor recognizes that body language is an important element in the communication process.

15. Diversity training is not a component of intercultural communications.

16. **Proxemics** refers to the nonverbal communication conveyed through voice pitch, volume, and inflection.

CHAPTER 4 Motivation—A Prerequisite for Success

LEARNING OBJECTIVES

1. Describe the motivation cycle.
2. Define motivation.
3. Identify the elements of a motivational plan.
4. Compare physiological needs with security needs.
5. List the items indicating a strong esteem need.
6. Describe how an officer can become self-actualized.
7. Compare satisfiers and dissatisfiers.
8. Describe Theory X and Theory Y.
9. Identify the four basic assumptions that underpin the expectancy theory.
10. Define the term valence.
11. Describe the concept of psychological success.

KEY TERMS

- achievement–motivation
- behavior modification
- dissatisfiers
- ends
- esteem
- expectancy motivational model
- expectancy theory
- facet feelings
- global feelings
- human behavior
- hygiene
- job satisfaction
- means
- motivation cycle
- motivators
- physiological needs
- psychological needs
- satisfiers
- security needs
- self-actualized needs
- sensitivity
- social needs
- Theory X–Theory Y
- valence

Chapter Summary

I Why Officers Work?

Determining the basic human needs is fundamental to understanding human behavior. **Human behavior** does not just happen—it is caused. Behavior follows a pattern showing:

1. A need will mobilize the energy to reach an acceptable goal.

2. As the need increases in intensity, goal attainment becomes emphasized by the individual.

3. As the need increases, behavior will follow, which, hopefully, will allow the individual to attain the goal.

A. Motivation Cycle. Motivation is a continuous process consisting of three specific steps:

1. Need. An individual experiences a need caused by external or internal forces, and those forces become mobilized.

2. Responding behavior. A responding behavior occurs, and energy intensifies and satisfaction occurs.

3. Goal. A goal is reached.

An individual's motivation depends on two factors: the strength of the need and the belief that a certain action will lead to need satisfaction. The intensity of an individual's motivation depends on the perception of the real value of the goal.

A supervisor has a direct responsibility to motivate employees and to provide a work environment, leading to officer satisfaction. He or she must create conditions to maximize the productivity of officers while department goals are achieved. A supervisor should create an atmosphere of consistency in a style where most officers become self-motivated. Toward these **ends,** the supervisor should develop an achievement–motivation program.

II Needs-Based Motivation

Abraham Maslow's theory on the hierarchy of needs (Figure 4.4) is one of the most widespread motivational theories in use. He stated that (1) an individual's needs are complex and hierarchical and (2) the best individuals (purportedly 1 percent of the population) are self-actualized. Maslow believed that a human being constantly wants something. As soon as one desire is satisfied, another takes its place.

A. **Physiological Needs.** These are the strongest and most fundamental needs that sustain life, that is, food, shelter, sex, air, water, and sleep. Deciding the degree to which officers are motivated by physiological needs is important for a supervisor. Concentrating on these needs for motivation is to concentrate on financial rewards.

B. **Security Needs.** This is primarily the need for reasonable order and stability with freedom from being anxious and insecure. Supervisors must realize that some officers enter police work because government agencies provide a secure and stable job. These officers want stability and predictability above all else. Security-minded officers want everything in black and white. Management that wants to meet security needs can emphasize traditional union demands and limit complex problem-solving situations or any type of risk taking.

   Management must identify the supervisor's need for security as well. A supervisor driven by security needs will be well-organized, rigid, and will strive above all else to please and placate the higher chain of command. This supervisor may ignore the needs of the subordinates and use manipulation when necessary. He or she often believes that subordinates have no need to control their own lives.

   Individuals should examine their own security needs through the following questions:

   1. How far would you go to cover up personal mistakes?
   2. Would you cover up mistakes made by supervisors?
   3. Would you do anything just to get promoted?
   4. Do you always agree with the boss just because that person is the boss?

C. **Social Needs.** An individual needs to have affiliation with others, a place in the group. If social needs are not fulfilled by the organization, an officer will often respond by an excessive use of sick time and low productivity.

   When a supervisor identifies that social needs are the motivating needs, the supervisor should promote social interaction for those officers. This can be done through things such as workout rooms, parties, or sporting activities.

   Management needs to monitor socially motivated supervisors, as they will emphasize the officers' needs and will ignore the organizational needs. Individuals should examine their own social needs through the following questions:

   1. When you become a supervisor, can you change roles and lead?
   2. How strong is your need to be socially accepted?
   3. When you are promoted, can you accept being a part of management?

D. **Esteem Needs.** Self-esteem needs include the need for independence, freedom, confidence, and achievement. Needs for respect from others include the concepts of recognition, prestige, acceptance, status, and reputation.

   Officers who do not believe their *esteem* needs are being fulfilled by their job will become disgruntled employees. Supervisors should try to recognize their subordinates for a job well done. A supervisor driven by esteem will usually be a good manager, as they will drive themselves with deep intensity to be recognized.

E. **Self-Actualization.** This is the stage when an individual has the need to develop feelings of growth and maturity. He or she becomes increasingly competent and gains a mastery over situations. Motivation is totally internalized and requires no external stimulation. This person usually focuses on being creative and constructive in work situations. When a supervisor recognizes an officer driven by self-actualization, that officer should be included in special assignments that will allow him or her to be creative, such as taskforces.

III *Motivational–Hygiene Theory*

Frederick Herzberg and colleagues developed the motivational–hygiene theory, which was based on their study of **job satisfaction**.

A. **Motivators.** These factors relate to the work itself and revolve around things such as achievement, advancement, recognition, and responsibility. It is primarily the motivators that result in job satisfaction.

B. **Hygiene Factors.** These factors are generally related to work conditions and policies, including things such as interpersonal relations, salary and benefits, job security, and working conditions. Hygiene factors are generally related to feelings of unhappiness.

See Figure 4.7 to compare and contrast Maslow's and Herzberg's theories.

IV *Theory X–Theory Y*

Theory X–Theory Y, developed by Douglas McGregor, is based on the belief that managers conduct themselves according to their assumptions, generalizations, and hypotheses about human behavior.

Theory X was the prevalent management style for law enforcement in the early days. It is the traditional view of direction and control, and stresses that:

1. The average employee actually dislikes work and will do whatever is necessary to avoid it.

2. If employees dislike work, most employees will have to be coerced, controlled, directed, or threatened with punishment in order to accomplish the organizational objectives.

3. Security is important to the average employee. This employee has little ambition and would rather be told what to do.

Theory X places emphasis on control and direction. Procedures are created for providing officers with close supervision and the creation of a **means** for providing rewards and punishments.

Theory Y appears to apply to the motivation of employees who have developed a social esteem or self-actualization need. Theory Y stresses:

1. Most employees will respond as positively to work as they do to play or rest.

2. Control and direction are not the only techniques to achieve departmental goals. When committed to departmental goals, employees will have self-control and self-direction.

3. Commitment to departmental objectives is a function of the rewards associated with the attainment of objectives.

4. Avoidance of responsibility, an accentuation on security, and limited drive are consequences of experience, not fundamental characteristics of human nature.

5. The ability to exercise a high degree of imagination, ingenuity, and creativity when striving to solve an organizational problem is a talent distributed among the population.

6. With industrial life conditions as they are, the intellectual potential of the average employee is used only partially.

The application of Theory Y reduces the need for external control and relies on other managerial techniques for reaching organizational goals. Supervisors should view officers as assets and develop interpersonal relationships.

V Expectancy Theory

Victor Vroom documented the expectancy theory.

A. Expectancy Theory. This theory is based on the concept that internal state and external forces impinging upon an individual will enable the person to act in a specific manner. A worker will be motivated to do what is required of him or her when it will lead to certain desired goals. With this theory, behavior is a product of the vitality of an individual and the environment, and individuals will develop preferences for available objectives. Employees have expectancies about outcomes.

Psychological Success. Psychological success as a means to increase self-esteem occurs when a personal challenging goal is set, methods of achieving that goal are set, and the goal is relevant to one's self-concept.

Valence. The strength of an individual's preference that an appropriate outcome will occur.

VI How to Motivate

Supervisors can use **behavior modification** to influence behavior to meet organizational objectives. Within this framework, officers will continue or repeat behavior with positive consequences and will cease behavior that has negative results.

If a supervisor uses positive reinforcement to modify behavior, it must be done continuously and consistently. Punishment of employees should be a last resort and not a supervisory style. A punishing style of leadership is a negative managerial style that causes employees to react defensively and reduces work productivity.

A supervisor should be encouraged to use reinforcement techniques to shape subordinates' behavior. However, reinforcement techniques must be response-contingent and utilized thoughtfully and systematically. That is why it is found that annual performance reviews usually prove ineffective in changing job behavior.

Multiple-Choice Questions (Circle the Best Answer)

1. Which of the following does not characterize the pattern that behavior will follow?

    a. A need will mobilize the energy to reach an acceptable goal.

    b. As the need increases in intensity, goal attainment is emphasized by the individual.

    c. As the need increases, behavior will follow that seems to be more promising for goal attainment.

    d. As the need increases beyond a certain level, the employee becomes fixated on the specific need and disregards the ultimate goal.

2. To become an effective supervisor, all of the following are true except:

    a. One must create the conditions that maximize the productivity of the officers.

    b. One must coordinate the officers' efforts so as to achieve departmental goals.

c. One must recognize that every officer is a unique individual, and, consequently, each individual is stimulated by differing needs.

d. One must recognize that officers can be motivated by fear.

3. The combination of _____ determines what motivates an officer to act in a certain way in a particular situation.

   a. internal factors and stress

   b. external and internal factors

   c. goals and objectives

   d. external factors and goals

4. A motivated employee is the product of the interaction of the employee with the _____ and the _____ that are generated.

   a. organization, attitudes

   b. work environment, actions

   c. supervisor, actions

   d. work, goals

5. The _____ is a vehicle aiding in the understanding of human behavior, which provides an appreciation of interacting forces and resultant behavior.

   a. psychological need

   b. satisfaction cycle

   c. motivation cycle

   d. human needs test

6. An officer who is placed with an organization that really motivates its employees will find all of the following to be true except

   a. there are identifiable goals.

   b. the culture can readily be identified with.

   c. tasks are accomplished easily.

   d. accomplished individuals are rewarded.

7. For many employees, the attainment of _____ is as important as material rewards.

    a. awards

    b. work-related goals

    c. promotion

    d. a global view

8. According to More, which two types of feelings come into play when considering work?

    a. Personal and professional.

    b. Organizational and individual.

    c. Security and fulfillment.

    d. Global and facet.

9. Within a good workplace, the relationship between each employee and the organization is one of

    a. reliance.

    b. blind faith.

    c. trust.

    d. acceptance.

10. Based on Herzberg's view of satisfiers and dissatisfiers, hygiene factors

    a. cannot increase job satisfaction, but only affect the amount of job dissatisfaction.

    b. are not related to satisfiers and dissatisfiers.

    c. are directly proportional to job satisfaction.

    d. cannot be measured.

11. When an agency concentrates on physiological needs as a means of motivating officers, they place emphasis on

    a. interpersonal relationships.

    b. better working conditions.

c. physical fitness.

d. extracurricular events.

12. Closely paralleling Theory X is another motivational theory called the

    a. "do unto others" theory.

    b. "you can lead a horse to water" theory.

    c. necessary evil theory.

    d. carrot and stick theory.

13. Hygiene factors are generally

    a. long-lived.

    b. short-lived.

    c. not adaptable.

    d. immeasurable.

14. Theory X places a strong emphasis on

    a. control and direction.

    b. control and relaxation.

    c. direction and relaxation.

    d. control and intimidation.

15. According to More, when officers are on probation and new to the job, a _____ approach may be more appropriate to supervise them.

    a. Theory X

    b. Theory Y

    c. Theory X–Theory Y

    d. None of the above

16. Which of the following features is not a part of the expectancy theory?

    a. Behavior is not determined exclusively by the individual.

    b. Employees have expectancies about outcomes.

    c. Effort–performance.

d. Performance–input.

e. Performance–outcome.

17. When reinforcement is used to modify behavior, it must be done

    a. consistently and continuously.

    b. as needed.

    c. by an analysis of each scenario and then a determination of action and method.

    d. differently, on an individual assessment basis.

True or False Questions

1. An individual's motivation to act depends on two factors: the strength of the need and the belief that a certain action will lead to need satisfaction.

2. A supervisor should strive to create a quality of organizational working life, in which most officers become self-motivated.

3. As a supervisor, it is your responsibility to develop needs in your officers, and, when appropriate, make organizational needs overcome personal needs.

4. Herzberg's study found that hygiene factors (i.e., job security, working conditions, salary, and benefits) were unrelated to the actual accomplishment of work.

5. Motivation is defined as an action that causes someone's behavior to change.

6. An agency where conditions are maximized for positive motivation is a department where one is allowed to be creative and accept a challenge.

7. The socially motivated supervisor stresses officers' needs and will ignore organizational needs.

8. The most widespread motivational theory in use is that developed by Victor H. Vroom.

9. Supervisors who recognize the importance of esteem need do everything possible to ensure that officers demonstrate self-confidence.

10. A supervisor whose primary drive is esteem will usually be a poor supervisor.

11. The self-actualized individual has a need to demonstrate the ability to assume responsibility and involvement at the highest possible level.

12. According to McGregor, the worker must be encouraged to develop to their highest capacity, acquire knowledge, and acquire skills.

13. One factor necessary for motivating employees is for the supervisor to understand that it is the supervisor's perception that counts, not the officer's.

14. According to More, the successful supervisor will concentrate on helping officers to clarify their needs and become aware of how officers perceive those needs.

15. Punishment is viewed as the quickest and most effective way of obtaining compliance.

16. A punishing style of leadership requires that the supervisor operates continuously from a positive managerial style.

17. If reinforcement is utilized before the desired behavior, it will not shape behavior.

18. Positive reinforcement rarely helps in changing performance outcomes.

19. The key to motivation is integration of the employee into the organization.

CHAPTER 5 Leadership—The Integrative Variable

LEARNING OBJECTIVES

1. Describe the skills required of a first-line supervisor.
2. Define leadership.
3. Compare legitimate and expert power.
4. Identify the limitations of coercive power.
5. List the traits a large police department has identified as qualities required of a good supervisor.
6. Identify the five groups of traits found to be associated with leadership effectiveness.
7. Compare initiating structure and consideration.
8. Describe the three major components of the contingency model of leadership.
9. Compare directive and participative leadership behavior.
10. Identify the three leadership mistakes.
11. Identify the four critical tasks that the leaders need to achieve in high-performance operations.

KEY TERMS

- attributes
- authority
- coercive power
- consideration
- consultative
- contingency
- directive
- expert power
- extending power
- high control
- initiating structure
- leadership
- leadership continuum
- leadership traits
- legitimate power
- low control
- moderate control
- operational skills
- participative
- personal relationships
- policy
- position power
- referent power
- relationship-oriented
- reward power
- task structure
- task-oriented leadership

Chapter Summary

The authors identify the most important characteristic of a well-managed department as leadership. Management has the responsibility to monitor its supervisors to make sure they are competent and ensure that the officers are not subjected to exploitative leadership by first-line supervisors. A person becoming a supervisor must shift from an **operational skills** focus to a greater **consideration** of human and conceptual skills.

A. **Operational Skills.** These skills involve techniques, methods, and use of equipment.

B. **Human Skills.** Development of the ability to understand why people behave the way they do in order to effectively change, direct, and control behavior. These skills involve motivation, communication, and direction.

C. **Conceptual Skills.** Development of one's knowledge of the overall organization and awareness of how the unit fits into the organization will allow the supervisor to work toward the attainment of the organizational goals and increased efficiencies.

Effective leadership leads to the accomplishment of clearly defined tasks. Four roles are critical to effective leadership:

1. Directional setter.
2. Change agent.
3. Spokesperson.
4. Coach.

D. **Leadership.** The process of influencing group activities toward the achievement of goals.

The first-line supervisor is no longer a doer, but a coordinator of other people's activities. Supervisors operate from a **position** of **power** based on the **authority** delegated to the supervisor. Supervisory power sources can be positional or personal.

I Power

According to More, first-line supervisors can extend power by using the following techniques:

1. **Persuasion.** A technique that has the supervisor communicate the reason and justification when exerting influence over others.

2. **Patience.** A technique that has the supervisor showing consideration to the shortcomings and weaknesses of each employee and balancing these against an immediate desire to attain objectives.
3. **Enlightenment.** Development of the ability to accept and value the insights, discernment, and seasoning of subordinates.
4. **Openness.** The ability to accept officers for who they are now and for what they can become as growth occurs. Requires accurate awareness of goals, values, desires, and intentions.
5. **Consistency.** Doing what is expected of you, so that your subordinates will always know where you are coming from and never have to feel as though they are being manipulated.
6. **Integrity.** Striving for control that can only be interpreted as fair, impartial, and nonmanipulative.

Supervisors exhibit honesty and real concern.
Positional and personal power can be further divided into five categories (Figure 5.2).

A. **Legitimate Power.** Power that comes from **policy** and written **directives** outlining a supervisor's authority and responsibilities.
B. **Expert Power.** Power that comes from the subordinates' knowledge that the supervisor possesses a greater amount of knowledge.
C. **Referent Power.** Power that is associated with the leader's personality. Sometimes identified as charisma, it is a quality that makes the supervisor likable.
D. **Coercive Power.** Power that is based on fear and the knowledge that the supervisor has the ability to administer some type of punishment.
E. **Reward Power.** Power that comes from being able to reward employees in some way. Power should be viewed with positive attitudes and not abused. Each type of power has its limitations.

II *Theories of Leadership*

A. **Trait Theory.** Identifies the distinguishing qualities or characteristics a person possesses when functioning as an effective leader. One researcher has identified five groups of traits associated with leadership effectiveness: (1) capacity, (2) achievement, (3) responsibility, (4) participation, and (5) status.

B. **Behavioral Theory.** Based on the Ohio State leadership studies that showed there are two types of leadership behavior:

1. **Initiating Structure.** The leader's behavior in delineating the relationship between himself/herself and his/her subordinates and attempting to establish well-defined patterns of organization, channels of communication, and methods or procedures.

2. **Consideration.** The leader's behavior indicative of friendship, mutual trust, respect, and warmth in the relationship between the leader and all members.

C. **Contingency Model.** Holds that the leader's style must match the demands of the specific situation. Fred Fiedler and associates developed the first contingency model, identifying three factors of importance:

1. **Position Power.** The degree to which the position itself confers upon the leader—the capacity to get officers to accept and comply with directions.

2. **Task Structure.** The extent to which a task is routine and structured as compared to an ambiguous and poorly defined task. When tasks are defined carefully, it is much easier for a supervisor to control operational duties and officers can be held responsible.

3. **Personal Relationships.** When the relationship between subordinates and a leader can be described as good, the supervisor is in a good position to influence behavior due to trust.

Fiedler identified two basic styles of leadership:

1. Task-oriented.
2. Relationship-oriented.

A leader's power can run from high position power (mutual trust and respect with highly structured tasks) to weak position power (little respect or support with vague tasks).

III Leadership Continuum

The relationship between a supervisor and subordinates exists along a continuum. Some researchers limit leadership style to two types (autocratic and democratic), whereas others identify more (e.g., authoritarian, democratic, laissez-faire, bureaucratic, and charismatic). Regardless of the number of styles, no supervisor sticks to one style. Usually, the supervisor adapts his or her style to meet the needs of individual situations.

More and Miller describe three types of leadership behavior when the supervisor wants to influence the behavior of line officers:

1. **Directive** is when a supervisor exhibits little concern for officers and allows little or no involvement in the decision-making process. A directive leader uses the authority of the position to attain subordinate obedience. This supervisor uses rules and regulations to ensure compliance.

2. **Consultative** is a leadership style of compromise when a supervisor shows concern for officers and their needs and also organizational needs. Subordinates are allowed to participate in the decision-making process when it results in a better decision.

3. **Participative** is when the supervisor has genuine belief and respect for subordinates. He or she fosters two-way communication, consulting with subordinates and involving them in the decision-making process. Group involvement is sought, and power is shared.

IV   Leadership Mistakes

Supervisors work for both management and subordinates. They are responsible not only to tell the officers what to do, but to also coach them when circumstances require it and to consult with them and join with them to attain objectives. Delegation is essential. The misuse of power by a first-line supervisor may prove useful initially, but over a long period can lead to the downfall of a first-line supervisor. It is important to accept individual differences and work with employees to make them the best they can be. Supervisors must be fair.

Multiple-Choice Questions (Circle the Best Answer)

1. According to the nationwide survey cited in the text,
    a. the chart of the typical police organization is constricted in the middle, where the number of sergeants is outweighed by both line officers below them and the ranks of lieutenant, captain, and major above them.
    b. a typical police organization can be diagrammed by an inverted pyramid.
    c. in a typical police organization, first-line supervisors outnumber managers in all other administrative positions.
    d. none of the above.

2. Sergeants need to divide their time between doing and managing, which can be referred to as

    a. the rule of coordination.

    b. the rule of balance.

    c. the 50 percent rule.

    d. none of the above.

3. Supervisory skills include

    a. operational, human, and conceptual.

    b. position and power.

    c. direction, delegation, and discussion.

    d. tasks and relationships.

4. Positional power sources include

    a. expert, reward, coercive.

    b. legitimate, coercive, reward.

    c. referent, expert.

    d. coercive, referent, expert.

5. Personal power sources include

    a. expert, reward, coercive.

    b. legitimate, coercive, reward.

    c. referent, expert.

    d. coercive, referent, expert.

6. The theories of leadership can be grouped into which three categories?

    a. Trait theories, behavioral theories, contingency theories.

    b. Trait theories, individual theories, group theories.

    c. Individual theories, behavioral theories, group theories.

    d. Individual theories, behavioral theories, contingency theories.

7. Ralph Stogdill identified a group of traits associated with leadership effectiveness, which includes

   a. capacity, achievement, and power.

   b. capacity, responsibility, and power.

   c. power, status, and achievement.

   d. status, responsibility, and capacity.

8. The behavioral model identifies two basic types of leadership behavior, which are

   a. initiating structure and resolution.

   b. resolution and consideration.

   c. consideration and initiating structure.

   d. none of the above.

9. A supervisor who feels comfortable emphasizing consideration is likely to use

   a. one-way communication and emphasize high standards.

   b. one-way communication and show that there is mutual trust.

   c. two-way communication and show respect for officers' ideas.

   d. two-way communication and carefully plan activities.

10. A supervisor who has activities carefully planned and communicated, has deadlines established, and gives instructions is said to be emphasizing

    a. consideration structure.

    b. resolution structure.

    c. initiating structure.

    d. none of the above.

11. Under the _____, first developed by Fred Fiedler and associates, the leader's style must match the demands of a specific situation.

    a. leadership continuum

    b. contingency model

c. behavioral model

d. consistency model

12. According to Fiedler, there are two basic styles of leadership, which are

    a. task-oriented, goal-oriented.

    b. goal-oriented, power-oriented.

    c. power-oriented, task-oriented.

    d. relationship-oriented, task-oriented.

13. For the newly appointed supervisor whose influence is limited, the leadership style that will be most effective is

    a. goal-oriented.

    b. power-oriented.

    c. task-oriented.

    d. relationship-oriented.

14. Interaction of the leadership style, extent of control, and the situational dimension result in a position whereby the relationship-oriented leader is most effective in a _____ situation, and the task-oriented leader is most effective in _____ or _____ situations.

    a. moderate control, high control, low control

    b. high control, low control, moderate control

    c. low control, moderate control, high control

    d. none of the above

15. In participative management, a manager _____ performs a task alone when it can be accomplished through the efforts of others.

    a. always

    b. seldom

    c. sometimes

    d. never

True or False Questions

1. Taking on a leadership position requires first-line supervisors to rely on their established view of themselves and to maintain a reliance on knowledge, methods, and techniques that have worked for them in a line position.

2. The move to a first-line supervisory position in law enforcement requires greater consideration of human skills.

3. The discharge of leadership responsibilities is a demanding role and forces a supervisor to make decisions and control behavior.

4. According to More, leadership is defined as the process of influencing personal activities toward the achievement of goals.

5. A knowledgeable supervisor who demonstrates the ability to implement, analyze, evaluate, and control situations and resolve problems is readily accepted.

6. The trait approach does not acknowledge the complex interaction between the actions of the leader and the situation.

7. Within trait theory, five groups of traits have been identified for leadership effectiveness, which include capacity, achievement, responsibility, communication, and status.

8. The concept of initiating structure defines the leader's behavior in delineating the relationship between leader and work group and in endeavoring to establish well-defined patterns of organization, channels of communication, and methods or procedures.

9. The concept of consideration defines the leader's behavior as being indicative of friendship, mutual trust, respect, and warmth in the relationship between leader and work group.

10. According to Fred Fiedler's theory of leadership, there are four factors of importance.

11. The contingency theory incorporates various indexes of power that include the leader's official rank and status and the leader's ability to recommend punishments and rewards.

12. When tasks are defined, it is much easier for a supervisor to control operational tasks, and officers can be held responsible for their actions or inactions.

13. According to Fiedler's theory, a structured task is enforceable, while the unstructured task is ambiguous and difficult or impossible to enforce.

14. There is no one style of leadership that will be successful all the time with everyone you are supervising.

15. Directive leadership advantages are focused on goal attainment and minimal compliance.

16. The consultative supervisor shows a concern for officers and their needs, as well as organizational needs.

17. "The decision involves the personal or work life of an officer and input is sought" demonstrates a consultative style of leadership.

18. Consultative leadership advantages are focused on minimal compliance and a limited effectiveness in solving problems.

19. A participative leadership style can only be utilized when the supervisor has a genuine belief in and respect for subordinates.

20. Participative leadership advantages are that employees are motivated and communication is improved.

CHAPTER 6 Team Building—Maximizing the Group Process

LEARNING OBJECTIVES

1. Describe the socialization process in a police department.
2. Prepare a short essay describing the relationship between the individual and the group.
3. Compare vertical and horizontal cliques.
4. Identify the characteristics of a random clique.
5. Describe the stages in the group development process.
6. List the elements constituting norms in a law enforcement agency.
7. Describe how a supervisor can build a winning team.
8. List the ways in which taskforces can be advantageous.
9. Describe the manner in which one should conduct a meeting.

KEY TERMS

- building a winning team
- cliques
- collaboration
- concept
- conducting meetings
- conform
- contribute
- controversy and conflict
- cooperation
- deadly force
- effective relationships
- formal groups
- group development process
- group development stages
- group norms
- group performance
- group problem solving
- groupthink
- horizontal cliques individual
- importance of the individual
- individual and the group
- informal groups
- interactions
- isolation
- law enforcement norms
- loyalty
- performance
- police culture
- preparation
- random cliques
- resolution
- role of the group
- silence
- size of the group
- stages of group development
- task force
- team building
- team goals
- team meetings
- vertical cliques

Chapter Summary

A supervisor must acquire an understanding and working knowledge of group dynamics.

A. Group. Consists of two or more people who interact with and influence each other for a common purpose. Two key factors to group dynamics are as follows:

1. Interaction.
2. Influence.

I The Individual

Socialization of a police agency is the means by which a new employee is indoctrinated into the organization. The new employee must adjust to the organization—the organization should never adjust to the **individual**.

The agency will generally require officers to acquire norms, values, and specific behavior developing from:

1. Organizational goals.
2. Approved means utilized to achieve goals.
3. Individual responsibility as defined by the agency.
4. Behavior patterns required as a part of **performance**.
5. Policies, rules, and regulations that maintain the organization.

The police academy emphasizes **conformity** and rejects individuality. Then, the field-training officer system brings the peer value system to the officer. These sorts of factors perpetuate the long-standing "us against them" mentality that isolates police from the community. Because of the changing demographics and standards of new officers, individuals are not adjusting as they have in the past, and the strong police identity has been weakened. However, the socialization process is still a factor in the development of commitment and **loyalty**.

II The Individual and the Group

Supervisors must realize that groups, whether formal or informal, will always exist within an organization. While many officers may work alone day-to-day, there are benefits to forming groups, such as building a sense of belonging, attachment to the agency, and a sense of stability. The supervisor's primary responsibility is to achieve results through people. The more information a supervisor can develop about the members of the group, the more effective the supervisor can be when working with the group. Groups can be destructive or supportive. Understanding group dynamics will enhance success.

III Role and Function of the Group

Knowing how a group functions usually leads to more effective problem solving.

A. **Formal Groups.** Created and supported by the organization for the express purpose of fulfilling specific organizational needs or performing special tasks. They are either temporary or permanent, depending on the needs of the organization.

B. **Informal Groups.** Evolve as a result of the formal organization being unable to meet all social or departmental officer requirements. These groups are rarely sanctioned by the formal organization, and they often cut across organizational lines. These groups can evolve into **cliques** and break down into three types. Cliques can lead to misunderstanding and hostility.

  1. **Vertical Cliques.** Generally occur in one unit of the department, usually between the first-line supervisor and the subordinates. The goal is to humanize the organization and reduce friction between the department and the officers. The supervisor protects underlings by disregarding errors and minimizing problems. The officers, in turn, protect the supervisor.

  2. **Horizontal Cliques.** Cut across departmental lines and will normally include many first-line supervisors. This clique prefers to work defensively and works most effectively when it is dealing with problems that may weaken authority or create some change that is adverse to the members' welfare. Usually more powerful than the vertical clique, it strives to maintain the status quo.

  3. **Random Cliques.** Rather than striving for change, its members merely desire to associate with other members of the department. Officers become members for the primary purpose of exchanging information. It is usually the primary source of rumors. This clique can be used to pass on information or as an information source. This group intensifies social relationships within the department.

IV Group Development Process

A newly organized group passes through six stages:

1. Orientation.
2. Conflict and challenge.

3. Cohesion.
4. Delusion.
5. Disillusion.
6. Acceptance.

As a group forms, members develop techniques to control the behavior of others. These techniques are called **group norms**. Norms are unwritten, but can be more powerful than organizational rules and regulations. They are powerful because they are backed by the power of the group. They develop through social interaction, and they provide continuity in the work environment, predictability of behavior that leads to a feeling of wellbeing, and the carrying out of routine procedures without disruption. **Law enforcement norms** include loyalty, secrecy, danger, **deadly force**, **isolation**, and performance.

V *Group Performance*

Supervisors must view working with the group as a challenge and should develop a positive attitude toward groups. Groups can have greater productivity because they allow officers to specialize and use their own special skills. They are a tool for bringing resources together to solve problems.

Group cohesiveness is important and generates a great degree of loyalty, identity, acceptance, and conformity. Cohesiveness is enhanced when the group attains its objectives successfully. Although group cohesiveness is a positive factor leading to high productivity, the negative side is the possibility of the group coming together and using its power to resist management.

VI *Building a Winning Team*

Team building is a complex process that requires a great deal of leadership and team effort. Supervisors must create an environment conducive to its members truly functioning as a team. Effectiveness of the group is influenced by factors such as size, norms, goals, and environment. Group leaders who are viewed as highly productive show similar characteristics. They:

1. Focus continuously on a goal.
2. Act as the leader to group activities while participating in the group.
3. Control the relationship between the group and other people or units.
4. Facilitate assumption of leadership roles when the situation dictates.

A supervisor should try to develop effective and positive personal relationships within a group. Then, the supervisor can seek out group members to obtain opinions and open communication. The supervisor should ask questions dealing with problems and not personalities. The larger the team, the more difficult it is to obtain esprit de corps and cohesiveness. The smaller the group, the greater the potential for interaction among members. It is recommended that teams be kept around ten members, and fewer than that when possible.

One of the supervisor's biggest challenges is to create sufficient opportunities for interaction, and officers' time should be scheduled to ensure adequate time for group interaction. Disagreements are normal, and it is important to focus on issues rather than personalities. When **controversy** occurs, it should be dealt with openly within the group. An effective supervisor should attempt to be aware of everything that is happening and deal with potential problems. This is best achieved through two-way communication and through listening. **Conflict** or potential conflict should be handled immediately.

VII *Team Goals*

The first-line supervisor is responsible for setting goals and directions for the team that are clear and meaningful. Priorities should be set with no room for misinterpretation. It is important that there be openness at all times, and all issues should be handled candidly. This will lead to the development of a cohesive group.

VIII *Group Problem Solving*

Group problem solving in police work is typically handled by means of a **taskforce**. Taskforces are usually temporary, focusing on one subject or problem. The role of the supervisor is to maximize the advantages of group decision-making to reach the best possible decision. Advantages of taskforces include:

1. Decision-making is improved.
2. Greater acceptance of decisions.
3. Coordination is improved.
4. Problems are viewed from a broader perspective.
5. Power is shared.

Taskforces are a good training mechanism for teaching officers to make decisions based on a consensus. A taskforce sets an atmosphere for power sharing.

A supervisor also needs to realize the disadvantages of a taskforce:

1. Biases of members can be intensified.
2. Excessive influence of individuals with rank or expertise.
3. Domination by individuals within the group.
4. Diffused responsibility.
5. Cost in terms of time and money.

IX Conducting Meetings

Meetings should begin with the establishment of ground rules—setting out the nature, frequency, and goals of the meetings. Consensus is integral to the success of the decision-making process. Supervisors should facilitate interaction and communication. **Groupthink** is a deliberating style that can be used when consensus is more important than arriving at the best solution.

Multiple-Choice Questions (Circle the Best Answer)

1. Groups that are created to fulfill specific organizational needs or perform special tasks are
   a. informal work groups.
   b. formal work groups.
   c. non-sworn staff groups.
   d. contract support groups.

2. Groups that cut across organizational lines and have common interests are
   a. informal work groups.
   b. formal work groups.
   c. non-sworn staff groups.
   d. contract support groups.

3. Which clique's goal is to humanize the organization and reduce friction between the department and the officers?
   a. Vertical.
   b. Horizontal.

c. Random.

d. Parallel.

4. The clique that includes a number of first-line supervisors and functions most effectively when it is dealing with problems that are perceived as weakening one's authority is

   a. vertical.

   b. horizontal.

   c. random.

   d. parallel.

5. The clique that assumes a defensive posture and only functions when the situation dictates that it must respond to ensure the status quo is

   a. vertical.

   b. horizontal.

   c. random.

   d. parallel.

6. The most critical stage of group development to the success of the group is

   a. orientation.

   b. conflict and challenge.

   c. cohesion.

   d. delusion and disillusion.

   e. acceptance.

7. Which stage occurs when each member of the group has received enough information to accept that the group objective and leadership are legitimate?

   a. Orientation.

   b. Conflict and challenge.

   c. Cohesion.

   d. Delusion and disillusion.

   e. Acceptance.

8. The stage at which the group becomes aware that everything is not moving smoothly and uncertainty enters the picture is

   a. orientation.
   b. conflict.
   c. cohesion.
   d. delusion.
   e. acceptance.

9. The stage at which the group fully accepts that they are on a treadmill and are going nowhere is

   a. conflict.
   b. cohesion.
   c. delusion.
   d. disillusion.
   e. acceptance.

10. _____ are techniques that members of a group develop to control the behavior of others.

    a. Rules
    b. Biases
    c. Attitudes
    d. Norms

11. Extensive rules and regulations serve to reinforce this norm, and specific sanctions apply to those who deviate from the expected behavior. Which norm is it?

    a. Loyalty.
    b. Belonging.
    c. Danger.
    d. Security.

12. Which of the following groups is distinguished from other groups because it is usually temporary and focuses attention on one subject or problem?

    a. Committee.

    b. Taskforce.

    c. Clique.

    d. Union.

13. According to the text, which two factors are important to the definition of a group?

    a. Size and competition.

    b. Interaction and influence.

    c. Belonging and purpose.

    d. Members and goals.

14. _____ into the police agency is the means by which rookies are transformed from civilian status to productive members of an operating agency.

    a. Initiation.

    b. Recruitment.

    c. Socialization.

    d. Actualization.

15. _____ can be important to the group and is the result of an officer's desire to be a member of the group and the degree of commitment felt by group members.

    a. Cohesiveness.

    b. Acceptance.

    c. Productivity.

    d. Esprit de corps.

True or False Questions

1. Types of informal groups include parallel, vertical, and random.

2. The horizontal clique serves a highly important function by intensifying social relationships within the department.

3. Groups serve as vehicles for decreasing personal relationships because social needs are satisfied more easily.

4. Groups that are cohesive can become an additional problem to first-line supervisors because they have more power than any single officer.

5. The advantage of a taskforce is that its final solution will be implemented because of the involvement of a cross-section of the department.

6. Advantages of a taskforce include power sharing and viewing problems from a broader perspective.

7. Within a police department, both formal and informal groups will always exist.

8. A supervisor's roles in team building are facilitator and developer.

9. Disadvantages of a taskforce include the following: bias of members can be intensified and cost in terms of time and money.

10. To maintain authority with a group, the supervisor should avoid any actual personal relationships with the group.

11. Efforts to improve officer safety has caused the number of officers killed or injured to decline.

12. Supervisors should intervene immediately when an officer engages in any type of risky behavior.

CHAPTER 7 Change—Coping with Organizational Life

LEARNING OBJECTIVES

1. Define change.
2. Describe what constitutes the process of change.
3. Identify the components of social values.
4. Describe the importance of police unions as a major component of the change process.
5. List the key elements of job satisfaction.
6. Describe the reasons officers accept change.
7. List what employees believe are unpopular decisions.
8. Describe how officers can participate in change.
9. Describe the pitfalls of mandated change.
10. Name the attributes of the police subculture.

KEY TERMS

- accepting change
- ambiguity
- code of silence
- cohesiveness
- cultural
- discretion
- fostering change
- habits
- informal leader
- job satisfaction
- loyalty
- mandated change
- protectors
- restricted relationships
- social values
- solidarity
- taboos
- technology
- unpopular decisions
- work values
- working for change

Chapter Summary

I Factors Fostering Change

Change is inevitable and an ongoing process that can be met with resistance or support. Change must be anticipated whenever possible. First-line supervisors deal with change on a daily basis. Dealing with change requires many skills, including communication, motivation, team building, and leadership. Change occurs in society, organizations, and individuals. Supervisors must recognize that there is a need to change leadership styles to fit with the changes occurring in policing.

II Police Unions

One result of changing values has been increased support of labor unions. Approximately 73 percent of the police officers in the United States are represented by a form of association or union. Police unions have been successful in allowing officers to (1) have an input in the future, (2) provide for some economic security, and (3) challenge the autocratic power of police managers.

A. Collective Bargaining. A process by which the department and the union negotiate a formal written agreement over wages, hours, and working conditions.

First-line supervisors definitely function as part of the management team, which separates them from officers in labor issues.

III The Law

Some problems facing police officers today include **ambiguity** and vagueness of the law, laws that are obsolete and outmoded, and political pressure that alters the enforcement of certain crimes. Such problems create frustration and job dissatisfaction in officers due to the spontaneous decision-making process that they are exposed to on the job. The officer must enforce the law and then accept the consequences if his or her decision is questioned.

IV Positive Aspects of Change

First-line supervisors interpret policies and serve as spokespeople for management. The sergeant whose style is objective and fair and shows concern for officers will find less resistance to change. A first-line supervisor is responsible for identifying the key variables within their subordinates that make the employee feel **job satisfaction**. These can include:

1. Accomplishment.
2. Accountability.
3. Advancement.
4. Challenge.

5. Comfort.
6. Compensation.
7. Management.
8. Relationships.
9. Resources.
10. Supervision.
11. Workload.

These are important to identify, as they can help the supervisor motivate subordinates and diffuse resistance to change.

Officers can be adaptable to change and will accept it more readily when included in the decision-making process. Reasons for **accepting change** include:

1. Choice.
2. Improvement.
3. Being informed.
4. A need is satisfied.
5. Planned change.

V *Resistance to Change*

Resistance to change can occur in many stages and for many reasons:

1. **Economic.** Wages and benefits that become threatened by either the chief administrators of the department or the politicians of the community will usually cause officers to unite, usually through associations or unions.

2. **Ambiguity created.** When the consequences of the change are either unknown or vague, there is a greater potential for resistance.

3. **Relationships restricted.** If management attempts to restrict the social relationships or change organizational structure, it is usually met with resistance.

4. **Habits altered.** People become used to doing things a certain way and may resist if forced to change from familiar work patterns and habits.

5. **Discretion restricted** *or eliminated.* Officers feel a sense of power when they utilize discretion and generally believe that excessive control over their discretion limits their effectiveness on the job.

6. **Unpopular decisions.** When unpopular decisions are being carried out, it is best to anticipate and prepare for resistance by providing justification for the decision.

7. **Cultural reasons.** Because the paramilitary background of law enforcement supports conformity, change is resisted merely because the organization itself fosters resistance to change.

VI *The Nature of Resistance*

A. **Rational Resistance.** Resistance to change may be valid. Rational resistance should be seen as a valuable part of the process of change because there might be a valid basis for resistance. By listening to officers' resistance, the supervisor can alter the change, which will develop trust and support of line officers if they know their opinion matters to management.

B. **Emotional Resistance.** Resistance is usually for individual reasons, especially those identified with job satisfaction.

   Deciding the basis for the resistance is important, so that change can be approached correctly and proper alterations can take place. The supervisor will have an advantage in dealing with change if he or she is a part of the management team and involved in the planning that precedes change.

C. **Being Knowledgeable.** A supervisor needs to be armed with all the information available before presenting the issue of change. It is imperative that each alternative be considered and each advantage or disadvantage be examined. Change must be "sold" to officers, so that resistance is reduced.

D. **Involvement.** If the persons who will be most affected by the change are asked to participate in the implementation phase of the change, it provides the greatest chance of success. It gives a message to the other officers to accept the change.

E. **Communication.** Keeping channels of communication open will provide useful information for "selling" change. Open communication reduces resistance and reduces the problems that can arise from rumors.

F. **Informal Leaders.** Informal leaders can often help implement change. They should be included in the process at the earliest stage of planning. They can influence the line officers because they are trusted.

G. **Mandated Change.** A first-line supervisor must be open and candid when mandated change is necessary. Supervisors should emphasize the positive aspects of change, reduce anxiety, and provide reliable information and a steadying influence. If the officers believe they can express their concerns to management, the resistance will be lessened.

Multiple-Choice Questions (Circle the Best Answer)

1. Change is
   a. static and cumulative.
   b. avoidable with proper planning.
   c. synergistic and cumulative.
   d. negative.

2. It is the quality of _____ that takes priority in satisfying the need system of officers.
   a. social life
   b. work life
   c. the labor agreement
   d. the resources

3. When _____ is pervasive, the greater the potential for resistance.
   a. secrecy
   b. ambiguity
   c. change
   d. unionization

4. The greater the _____, the more power that is taken away from the line officer.
   a. ambiguity
   b. restricted social interaction
   c. power of the union
   d. control of discretion

5. _____ serves to reduce resistance because the unknown becomes the known.
   a. Complete disclosure
   b. Involvement

c. Written regulation

   d. Mandated change

6. Resistance to change can be lessened

   a. as time passes and officers accept change.

   b. by mandating change.

   c. very little, as resistance to change is always expected.

   d. by integrating informal leaders.

7. _____ may be necessary when there is no time for or success with a consultative process of change.

   a. Mandated change

   b. Postponing change

   c. Absolute compliance

   d. Strict enforcement

True or False Questions

1. The larger and more bureaucratic a department is, the more it will resist change.

2. Police unions are viewed by line officers as a way to challenge the autocratic power of police managers.

3. Officers are adaptable to change and will accept it readily when involved in the decision-making process.

4. Reasons for the acceptance of change include improving work conditions and having a choice.

5. The resistance to change is usually individual and not collective.

6. There is no need for the supervisor to distinguish between rational and emotional resistance in order to effect a change.

7. To be effective in implementing change, a first-line supervisor must gather and assimilate the facts surrounding the change and identify the resistance leaders.

8. Efforts to restrict the flow of information can only enhance resistance to change and reinforce the informal organization.

9. Officers will normally resist change when it involves such things as restricted or eliminated discretion.

CHAPTER 8 Performance Appraisal—The Key to Police Personnel Development

LEARNING OBJECTIVES

1. Define the term labor-intensive.
2. Explore the function of performance appraisal.
3. Identify the characteristics of objective performance appraisals.
4. List the steps in the performance evaluation process.
5. Describe the roles and responsibilities of each actor in the performance evaluation process.
6. Examine the specific role of the police sergeant in performance evaluation.
7. Compare and contrast selected methods used to appraise on-the-job performance.
8. Describe errors that skew performance evaluations.
9. Describe both the purpose of and the dynamics involved in the appraisal interview.
10. Define remediation and follow-up in terms of the performance evaluation process.
11. Discuss the concepts of validity and reliability in performance appraisal.
12. Explore performance evaluation in the context of community-oriented policing.
13. Examine the emergence of trends related to appraising the performance of first-line police supervisors.

KEY TERMS

- a appraisal interview
- community-oriented policing
- cycle of evaluation
- employee assistance program
- errors
- evaluating supervisor performance
- evaluation interview
- evaluative methods
- follow-up
- frequency of evaluation
- goals and objectives
- institutional support
- neighborhood-oriented policing
- objective assessment
- objectivity, validity, reliability
- participation and empowerment
- performance appraisal
- performance evaluation
- performance measures
- personnel and productivity
- personnel development
- recency error
- remediation
- remediation
- roles and responsibilities
- sources of error
- supervisor's leading role

Chapter Summary

I Performance Appraisal

First-line supervisors' **responsibilities** include preparing **performance evaluations**, but few receive proper training on how to accomplish this task. Police managers recognize (1) that quality of service is likely to revolve around the recruitment and selection of **personnel** and (2) that important officer qualities include intelligence, ability, skill, experience, integrity, and dedication.

Management theorists believe that objective and fair performance appraisal systems enrich the relationship between the supervisor and the subordinate. Many human resource managers strongly believe that the real objective that a performance appraisal should meet is to inform employees about the quality of their work, so they might strive to improve their own performance.

A supervisor must know who is responsible for what and how the job is done. Performance appraisals should have certain characteristics:

1. Job centered with focus on a specific task(s).
2. Clear and simply stated.
3. Observable and objective.
4. Target actual on-the-job performance.
5. Measurable in terms of predetermined performance standards.

The four universal aspects of performance appraisals are as follows:

1. A performance goal, standard, or plan.
2. Measurement of job-related performance.
3. Comparison of employee performance with the goal, standard, or plan.
4. The use of corrective action.

Performance appraisals have been determined to be necessary by management to:

1. Allocate resources.
2. Reward competent employees.
3. Provide valuable feedback to workers.
4. Maintain fair relationships and communication bonds.

Officers, supervisors, and managers have distinct **roles** in the appraisal system, but unity of purpose is very important.

II Frequency of Evaluation

Formal evaluations should be performed on a schedule. If a supervisor evaluates an officer too frequently, the evaluator runs the risk of placing too much emphasis on normal day-to-day situations. If a superior evaluates an officer too infrequently, the risk is not remembering the critical incidents.

Probationary periods are valuable tools for quality control in the personnel screening process; however, there must be careful, consistent, and objective evaluations of the employee's on-the-job performance. Objective, thorough, and frequent performance appraisals ensure quality police service, protect the public, and promote professionalism.

III The Sergeant's Role

A first-line supervisor is the person usually responsible for the on-the-job performance evaluation of line personnel. Sergeants must realize that assessing a subordinate's job performance goes with the job and that how well it is done will depend on them. Being a good evaluator requires:

1. Natural talent.
2. Knowledge.
3. Acquisition of special skills.

Supervisors also require institutional support. They must be given management's support and be empowered with the authority to do a meaningful evaluation of subordinates. Management must train the supervisor properly and give access to needed department resources. When performance evaluations lack relevance, they can destroy the supervisor's morale and undermine the credibility of management.

Effective supervisors accept performance appraisals as a challenge and feel that it is worth taking risks because it offers them an opportunity to provide substance and form to the agency's resources. They help eliminate incompetent personnel and offer positive reinforcement to personnel who deserve it.

The three common objectives of personnel evaluations are as follows:

1. **Objective assessment.** To assess each employee's contribution to the organization.
2. **Appraisal interview.** To give employees valuable feedback concerning their performance.
3. **Remediation.** To develop a mutually acceptable plan for correcting any problems.

IV Methods of Appraisal

The text outlines a few of the more important methods of appraisal.

A. Graphic Rating Scale. This is done on a line scale to which the evaluator indicates the degree to which the person possesses the trait. The graphic scale ranges on a continuum from negative to positive. Advantages of this rating scale are that it is simple to design and construct, easy to use, easy to interpret, and employees can be compared based on a composite score. Disadvantages of this rating scale are rigidity, rater error, and the possibility of intentional manipulation skewing the results.

B. Critical Incident Method. Involves identifying, classifying, and recording significant employee behaviors, whether favorable or unfavorable. It requires three basic steps:

1. Accurate collection and documentation of the incidents.
2. Breaking the information into categories of significant job behaviors.
3. Providing the evaluator with a list of categories and a form on which to record an analysis.

C. Behaviorally Anchored Rating Scales (BARS). BARS are gaining popularity in the police area. This method focuses on specific on-the-job activities, rather than on personal traits. Sample statements are used to describe unacceptable, average, and excellent performance in representative incidents. The supervisor evaluates definite, observable, and measurable job behavior, choosing a numerical designation and incorporating these in a matrix configuration. While quite complex, adequate training and effective use make for a win–win situation.

D. Management by Objectives (MBO). MBO is a process designed to convert **goals and objectives** into specific programs. The employee and the first-line supervisor get together to map out future goals and objectives, measures of achievement, and time frames. On the next evaluation, the employee is evaluated on identified measures of achievement upon which the employee and supervisor previously agreed.

V The Human Factor

The integrity of the personnel assessment process is linked directly to the ability and skill of the sergeant. A first-line supervisor must be an impartial evaluator. In performance evaluations, there are opportunities for **errors**, which refer to influences that affect perceptions and interfere with objective assessment. Supervisors can be trained to recognize common errors in order to find ways to avoid them.

A. **Error of Leniency.** This is the most common error and involves the human tendency to give people the benefit of the doubt. This usually occurs due to supervisors wanting to be popular and to avoid interpersonal conflicts. It also protects one's ego from criticism. The error of leniency undermines the **objectivity** of the performance assessment process. Effective supervisors have to guard against allowing personal considerations to affect their evaluation of a subordinate.

B. **Error of Central Tendency.** It is placing the employees into an artificial category of "average." The error of central tendency affords the supervisor a process that makes him or her feel safe and will meet with the least amount of resistance by the employees. This error penalizes the highly motivated employee, while it rewards the marginal employee. The error destroys the credibility of the evaluation process and seriously affects employee morale.

C. **Error of the Halo Effect**. This error occurs when a supervisor allows one significant event or characteristic to be the basis for the overall rating of the employee. The evaluator then uses selective perception to justify the initial assessment.

   The error of related traits occurs when the evaluator assumes that an employee who exhibits one strength will automatically have others.

   The error of overweighting is when the supervisor is unduly influenced by a critical incident (positive or negative) near the end of the evaluation period.

D. **Error of Bias.** This error involves personal bias and is usually based on the supervisor's norms, values, prejudices, and operational stereotypes. Factors such as race, sex, sexual preference, creed, appearance, and lifestyle may affect the evaluation—whether intentionally or unintentionally. Supervisors are evaluating the person, rather than the on-the-job performance. Even when a supervisor does not like the individual employee, the evaluation should be fair and based on objective data.

E. **Contrast Error.** This error occurs when supervisors judge employees based on their own expectations and aspirations, rather than actual job performance. This emotion-based evaluation is subjective. If detected by employees, this error usually forces employees to guess what qualities or traits the supervisor is looking for and to gain approval through win-at-all-cost competitiveness or outright deception.

F. **Recency Error.** This error occurs when too much weight is placed on the employee's behavior immediately prior to the rating evaluation. Proper documentation throughout the evaluation period is essential in preventing overemphasis on easily recalled behaviors. Generally, recency error results in higher ratings, given that most subordinates are aware of the evaluation dates and adjust their behavior accordingly.

Supervisors who are trained properly in the evaluation process are the key to efficiency, effectiveness, and **productivity** in police work.

VI *Validity and Reliability of Performance Appraisal*

The objective of the performance assessment is to develop an accurate profile that will determine the competency of the personnel. It should identify individual capabilities and the employee's value to the organization. Therefore, **validity** and **reliability** of the evaluation are critical to the success of the process.

A. A valid performance appraisal should accurately measure the traits, applied problem solving, or goal attainment of the individual. The appraisal itself is an assessment of the degree to which a very specific accomplishment is related to a clearly stated performance standard. With a valid evaluation process, the measuring device will arrive at essentially the same result by any evaluator.

B. A reliable appraisal process measures appropriate job-related performance accurately and consistently each time it is used. This appraisal will not be biased by errors of the rater, manipulation by the employee, flaws in the measuring device, or constraints of time or place.

To overcome problems with a performance appraisal, the following actions may help to add to the reliability of the process:

1. Developing clear policies, procedures, rules, and regulations to govern the performance evaluation process.
2. Selecting a simple but valid performance appraisal instrument.
3. Training supervisors in gathering and interpreting objective evaluative data.
4. Active participation by the person being evaluated in all aspects of performance assessment.
5. A commitment by management to make personnel decisions on data obtained from formal performance appraisals.

VII *The Evaluation Interview*

After completion of the evaluation, results and recommendations should be communicated to the employee as soon as possible. The evaluation interview can be beneficial to the employee, sergeant, and organization.

The performance **appraisal interview** should be a forum for a positive face-to-face meeting between a supervisor and subordinate. It should result in collaborative problem solving and mutual goal setting. For it to be productive, the sergeant must be open and honest with the subordinate while still being helpful and supportive. The employee must be receptive and willing to cooperate by taking direction from the supervisor. The appraisal interview should explore the employee's strengths and weaknesses. It allows the supervisor the opportunity to offer positive reinforcement when appropriate and to address deficiencies and develop a plan to deal with them. The interview should be set up to focus the subordinate's attention on the future. To do this, the sergeant should conduct the interview in the following ways:

1. Discuss actual performance in detail, yet be tactful.
2. Emphasize strengths to build on.
3. Promote conforming to acceptable job performance.
4. Stress the opportunities that will allow the subordinate to grow personally while developing professionally.
5. Assist the subordinate in goal setting, with a few specific objectives that can be attained within a reasonable period while considering the available resources.

The interview should involve the following:

1. Evaluating.
2. Teaching.
3. Coaching.
4. Counseling.

The success of the interview depends largely on the supervisor's ability to establish rapport, empathize, and communicate effectively with subordinates. The interview should help the subordinate have an enthusiastic attitude about returning to work and a desire to improve on-the-job performance.

Performance appraisals and interviews must include remediation and **follow-up** in order to be effective.

VIII Remediation

A. Remediation. Using available resources to correct a personnel problem or remedy a deficiency. Supervisors normally deal with assessment and the appraisal interview, but the sergeant's role in remediation may be less direct. Sergeants usually deal directly with minor deficiencies or performance problems. If the subordinate's performance does not improve, the sergeant is responsible for recommending remediation, possibly through retraining, increasingly severe discipline, or termination from the agency.

Upper management is responsible for resolving serious or persistent performance problems. The sergeant's role then switches to one of advisor and information gatherer. **Employee assistance programs** (EAPs) are relatively new programs and play an important role in helping deviant, maladjusted, or marginal personnel who are capable of contributing to the organization. The sergeant can be trained to make preliminary diagnoses of the problem and make a referral to an EAP.

IX *Follow-Up*

It is the sergeant's responsibility to monitor the subordinate's progress toward reaching the mutually agreed-upon goals established during the performance interview. Without proper follow-up, the performance appraisal becomes meaningless. Appraisal should be a daily activity that becomes documented for the employee periodically as a performance evaluation. Follow-up is designed to motivate personnel and should lead to professional growth and development.

X *Changes in Trends*

Performance evaluations have become more positive and helpful and less negative or punitive for the subordinate. The supervisor clearly has the responsibility to lead subordinates to better performance, not to rule through fear and intimidation because of their position of authority. Two trends have emerged from an emphasis on participatory management: (1) evaluating officer performance under community policing and (2) subordinates **evaluating supervisor performance**.

Traditional performance evaluations are not geared to **community-oriented policing**. Modification through the following three steps will allow the process still to be effective:

1. Convey reasonable expectations concerning the content and style of police personnel behavior while reinforcing commitment to the department's mission, values, goals, and objectives.

2. Document the types of incidents that officers are experiencing in their communities and the problem-solving strategies they use to resolve problems.

3. Identify the organizational factors that hinder performance enhancement or the solicitation of ideas for dealing with changing conditions.

While many private enterprises have been having employees rate supervisors, the concept has been slow to develop in policing. Because there is so much that a supervisor does, which the subordinate cannot see, theorist Thomas Whetstone believes the appraisal should only be in the area of leadership. He also believes that employees should require training on how to evaluate the supervisor if the appraisal is going to offer any credible feedback and that officers should use a standard forced-choice instrument.

In order for the process to work effectively, it has to be structured to remove fear of retaliation and errors such as those discussed earlier. Management's commitment to the concept will go a long way toward success in supervisor evaluation. The ultimate goal is self-improvement.

Multiple-Choice Questions (Circle the Best Answer)

1. Many personnel specialists believe that a performance appraisal system should be limited to one objective, which is to

    a. inform employees about the quality of their work, so that they might strive to improve performance.

    b. show each employee how well the supervisor likes him or her.

    c. show how effective each officer is as a team player.

    d. demonstrate what behavior is unacceptable.

2. The most important elements of performance appraisal include all but which of the following characteristics?

    a. They are job centered.

    b. They are clear and simply stated.

    c. They are objective as well as subjective.

    d. They are observable.

    e. They are measurable in terms of a predetermined performance standard.

3. According to the text, a performance appraisal is necessary in order to do all of the following except

    a. allocate resources.

    b. reward competent employees.

    c. provide valuable feedback to workers.

    d. determine an officer's right to receive a merit raise and maintain fair relationships and communication bonds.

4. According to More and Miller, under ideal circumstances, police departments should require at least

   a. 2 years of probation, with rookie police officers evaluated every 6 months.
   b. 1 year of probation, with rookie police officers evaluated every month.
   c. 18 months of probation, with rookie police officers evaluated every 3 months.
   d. 1 year of probation, with rookie police officers evaluated every 6 months.

5. Performance evaluations have three common objectives, which include all of the following except

   a. assessment.
   b. evaluation interview.
   c. remediation.
   d. counseling.

6. Methods of appraisal include all but which of the following?

   a. Graphic rating scale.
   b. Critical incident method.
   c. BARS.
   d. MBO.
   e. Total quality management.

7. The critical incident method advantage is that

   a. it deals with hypothetical situations.
   b. it zeroes in only on positive aspects of behavior.
   c. it is well suited for the employee-counseling aspect of performance assessment.

8. When supervisors give the person the benefit of the doubt and evaluate the person higher than the circumstances warrant, they are guilty of the

a. error of leniency.

b. error of central tendency.

c. error of contrast.

d. error of bias.

9. According to More and Miller, the most common error in rating police personnel is the

a. error of leniency.

b. error of central tendency.

c. error of contrast.

d. error of bias.

10. When supervisors force many employees into an artificial category labeled "average," they are guilty of the

a. error of leniency.

b. error of central tendency.

c. error of contrast.

d. error of bias.

11. When the supervisor allows just one outstanding characteristic or critical incident to shape the overall rating, the supervisor is guilty of the

a. error of leniency.

b. error of central tendency.

c. halo effect.

d. error of bias.

e. error of contrast.

12. According to More and Miller, while the exact configuration varies from one department to the next, most formal employee evaluation systems have _____ steps.

a. three

b. five

c. nine

d. eleven

13. When supervisors have a tendency to rate the employees they know and really like much higher than can reasonably be justified by an objective assessment of performance, they are guilty of the

    a. error of leniency.

    b. error of central tendency.

    c. error of contrast.

    d. error of bias.

14. Because much of a supervisor's work is not observed by employees, the supervisor evaluation should focus on

    a. leadership issues.

    b. personality.

    c. team spirit.

    d. productivity.

15. _____ penalize(s) competent, achievement-oriented employees and reward(s) marginal employees.

    a. Favoritism

    b. Personal politics

    c. Average evaluations

    d. Self-fulfilling prophecy

16. When supervisors tend to judge subordinates in terms of their own expectations and aspirations, they are guilty of the

    a. error of leniency.

    b. error of central tendency.

    c. error of contrast.

    d. error of bias.

17. The performance appraisal interview benefits

    a. the employee.

    b. the supervisor.

    c. the agency.

    d. all of the above.

18. A performance evaluation that is an accurate measurement of the traits, applied problem solving, or goal acquisition the evaluation purports to measure is said to be

    a. valid.

    b. reliable.

19. A performance evaluation that is not biased by the idiosyncrasies of the rater, manipulation by the evaluate, flaws in the design of the measuring device, or the constraints of time or place is said to be

    a. valid.

    b. reliable.

True or False Questions

1. Systematic performance appraisal is regarded as the key to employee development and is viewed as the centerpiece of an effective police personnel system.

2. The universal aspects of performance appraisal are the use of corrective action as required in a given situation and the measurement of job-related performance.

3. Not everyone has the inclination and/or talent to be a good evaluator.

4. Being a good evaluator requires natural talent and acquisition of special skills.

5. Influences that distort perceptions and interfere with an objective assessment are halo effect, errors of leniency, central tendency, and bias.

6. Reliability of performance appraisal is somewhat easy to achieve.

7. Institutional support is not essential for a performance appraisal program to be effective.

8. Graphic rating scales are tricky performance assessment devices because interpretation is quite difficult.

9. A constructive performance assessment interview focuses the subordinate's attention on the future, rather than the past.

10. The EAP movement assumes that it is better to "cut losses" with problem employees, rather than try to salvage them with costly intervention.

11. According to theorist Thomas Whetstone, officers conducting supervisor evaluations should remain anonymous, so that they can be totally honest without fear of retaliation.

12. Clarity and specificity are essential components of MBO.

CHAPTER 9 Training, Coaching, Counseling, and Mentoring—Helping Officers Grow and Develop

LEARNING OBJECTIVES

1. Learn how to communicate with officers by emphasizing listening.
2. Learn how to establish a positive working relationship with officers.
3. Learn the importance of knowing the mission, goals, and values of the organization.
4. Understand the value of providing positive feedback.
5. Understand your limitations for being a positive influence.
6. Describe how the "coach's" values affect the learning curve of officers.
7. Describe the qualities needed to be an effective supervisor and coach.
8. Understand the need for listening versus speaking in order to become a successful supervisor/coach.
9. Describe the different styles of counseling and how they differ.
10. Describe the variables of the effective counseling process and how they interact.
11. Describe mentoring "pitfalls" that need to be avoided.

KEY TERMS

- andragogy
- atmosphere
- beliefs
- combined style
- commitment
- constructive feedback
- counseling errors
- counselor
- developmental counseling
- directive style
- documentation
- empowerment
- field-training officer
- flexibility
- goals
- involvement
- listening keys
- loyalty
- mentee
- mentor
- mentoring
- mission
- nondirective style
- operational climate
- optimistic feedback
- pitfalls
- principles
- retention level
- role model
- self-confidence
- self-development
- self-image
- teach technical skills
- techniques
- training
- two-way communication
- values
- vicarious liability
- vision

Chapter Summary

Working in an imperfect world is a challenge that a first-line supervisor must accept; consequently, a supervisor should work diligently at creating a positive working environment. First-line supervisors must learn to manage as a coach/counselor/mentor. Coaching is a positive process that places a supervisor in a position to help officers perform more effectively. When officers are coached correctly, they become committed to the **mission** and **goals** of the department.

In today's working environment, coaching can be used to accomplish a wide range of tasks, including making it clear what the organization's performance expectations are, to allowing an officer to attain individual goals. An effective coach creates a work environment that allows him or her to work with and help officers grow and develop.

Supervisors who follow the principles of coaching/counseling/mentoring can provide a frame of reference in which an officer will have the capacity to realize their true potential. These principles range from really understanding oneself to communicating by emphasizing listening. A supervisor must assess him- or herself, realizing that weaknesses and strengths must be addressed, as they commit themselves to coaching. A coach must work assiduously at becoming aware of their own attitudes, beliefs, biases, frustrations, values, and opinions, so that they will not negatively influence their effectiveness as a coach.

When a supervisor consistently strengthens the department value system, it provides officers with a reason for organizational existence and informs officers what they have to do and why. When a coach communicates honestly and reinforces agency values sincerely, a message of trust is conveyed to subordinates. A coach and subordinates can benefit from the creation of a positive work environment that encourages subordinate participation in decision-making, allows subordinates to become an integral part of the agency, and allows officers to work within the frame of reference of a definitive and comprehensive value system.

Relationship is the foundation of coaching. It is the process of influencing the actions of others in such a way that the outcomes are mutually satisfying to everyone concerned. This is done through communicating and motivating. The creation of a positive relationship between a coach and a subordinate reinforces organizational intent and purpose. Coaches have to be conversant in organizational values. They are the reason an organization exists. They are more abstract than rules and regulations, they set the organizational tone, and they convey meaning that guides an officer's behavior.

The best coaches actually listen. Of special importance are the effective **listening keys** that range from being flexible to keeping an open mind. It is important to acknowledge that the more a supervisor talks, the less effective they become; thus, **two-way communication** reverts to one-way communication. Active listening has been identified as the most effective means of listening. This is done when the coach shows an understanding—verbally—when interacting with an officer.

A good coach has the ability to train officers either as a team or individually. A skillful coach realizes that learning by experience can take a long time and that officers may need individual instruction or advice to accomplish an objective by approaching a problem differently or using an entirely different technique.

Feedback is a compelling coaching skill, which is especially true when it involves an evaluation of actual performance. **Constructive feedback** can be of two types—optimistic or corrective—when dealing in the realm of performance coaching. **Optimistic feedback** is optimal and a goal that a coach should work toward. It is an ongoing process by which information can be shared freely and without restraint. However, **constructive feedback** is tailored to tell an officer that performance improvement is necessary.

A supervisor should be a role model for those supervised. A resonant role model energizes every supervised employee, which is especially true when a supervisor performs in an upbeat and positive manner. As a role model, a supervisor should be constantly engaged in a learning process and should transmit newly acquired knowledge to subordinates.

A counselor should strive to develop a working environment that is open, trusting, ethical, and built upon a foundation of integrity. One should demonstrate the willingness to work with officers and listen to their concerns about work-related and personal problems when the occasion arises. A counselor should continually stress the need for inculcating the norms, values, and ethics into the operational aspects of the department. **Involvement** and accountability are two very important aspects of building organizational **commitment**.

Developmental counseling is a subordinate-centered course of action that produces a plan outlining actions necessary for subordinates to achieve individual or organizational goals. It is strictly developmental in nature and is nonpunitive. A successful counseling style involves communication, flexibility, intention, and support.

The styles of counseling include directive, nondirective, and combined. Each style has advantages and disadvantages. An effectual counselor will use every possible technique to set the moral tone and perform counseling that results in goal attainment. When time allows, the combined approach stresses that planning and decision-making are the responsibility of the subordinate.

The counseling process takes into consideration atmosphere, time, documentation, and the counseling session. There are numerous ways to improve counseling—from being objective to encouraging the officer to take initiative. **Counseling errors** that should be watched for include acknowledging and controlling personal bias and keeping one's emotions under control.

Mentoring is relatively new to law enforcement and is defined as the proactive development of each subordinate by observation, assessment, coaching, teaching, developmental counseling, and evaluation. The **pitfalls** of mentoring range from not keeping officers informed to failure to delegate.

Multiple-Choice Questions (Circle the Best Answer)

1. Teaching focuses primarily on the improvement of _____ skills.

    a. technical and tactical

    b. human and affective

    c. conceptual and developmental

    d. affective and conceptual

    e. mentoring and counseling

2. Mentoring is a/an _____ process.

    a. exclusive

    b. optional

    c. inclusive

    d. evaluative

    e. teaching

3. One study found that to best influence patrol officer's behavior, supervisors must

    a. limit intervention to internal factors.

    b. reduce conflict.

    c. "do what I say, not what I do."

    d. provide extrinsic rewards.

    e. lead by example.

4. _____ give(s) substance to one's personal and professional self.

    a. Truthfulness

    b. Integrity

c. Values

d. Frankness

e. Honesty

5. Mentoring is

   a. very time-consuming.

   b. not as time-consuming as many anticipate.

   c. limited to selected officers.

   d. the refutation of disagreement.

   e. the rejection of imperfection.

6. A mentoring pitfall is

   a. too much praise.

   b. accepting too much input from subordinates.

   c. criticizing.

   d. controlling information.

   e. relying on other supervisors.

7. A feature of dedication is

   a. autonomy.

   b. resolution.

   c. sustained energy.

   d. too much initiative.

   e. too much delegation.

8. Officers look forward to exercising

   a. freedom from discipline.

   b. controlled direction.

   c. uniqueness.

   d. self-control.

   e. power.

9. Coaching is a/an _____ process.

   a. neutral

   b. positive

   c. leveling

   d. off-putting

   e. nonmotivational

10. Obtaining results through the efforts of others is a/an _____ mandate.

    a. actualization

    b. bureaucratic

    c. humanistic

    d. positional

    e. variable

11. A byproduct of the principles of coaching is

    a. one-way communication.

    b. understanding subordinates.

    c. restrictiveness.

    d. loyalty.

    e. self-assessment.

12. A coach should become aware of their own _____ that reinforce(s) or contradict(s) a spoken message.

    a. mien

    b. quirks

    c. appearance

    d. self-image

    e. autonomy

13. When an officer is allowed to make appropriate decisions, _____ follow(s).

    a. restrictions

    b. functionality

    c. imperativeness

    d. accountability

    e. creativeness

14. A good listener is one who

    a. exhibits an active body state.

    b. resists difficult expository.

    c. shows no energy.

    d. takes many notes.

    e. is intolerant of bad habits.

15. Active listening involves showing an understanding

    a. visually.

    b. by visualizing.

    c. by conceptualizing.

    d. by being judgmental.

    e. verbally.

16. The most skilled coach will diminish his or her impact by ignoring

    a. people skills.

    b. priorities.

    c. evaluative skills.

    d. gaps in knowledge.

    e. coping skills.

17. A coach who is in a position to identify _____ not realized by the individual being coached can improve the coaching process.

    a. techniques

    b. alternatives

    c. values

    d. rewards

    e. adversity

18. A coach should develop an attitude that allows for functional

    a. importance.

    b. morality.

    c. aptness.

    d. reduction.

    e. independence.

19. A developmental counseling effort identifies weaknesses and working with a subordinate on a/an _____ plan.

    a. functional

    b. operational

    c. execution

    d. achievement

    e. attainment

20. There are _____ features of a successful counseling style.

    a. two

    b. three

    c. four

    d. five

    e. six

True or False Questions

1. A supervisor does not have to deal with external imperfection.

2. First-line supervisors must learn to manage as a coach/counselor/mentor.

3. Human skills consume the smallest part of a supervisor's day.

4. Coaching cannot be viewed as a process.

5. Coaching has little to do with motivation.

6. Coaching is at the opposite end of a continuum from bureaucratic rules.

7. With coaching, officers can become increasingly self-sufficient.

8. Teaching skills and techniques is not a principle of coaching.

9. A coach should never pre-empt an officer by making decisions that should be made by the officer.

10. A coach's value system remains static.

11. Values are less abstract than rules and regulations.

12. The coaching process should not be used to reinforce the organization's value system.

13. The applications of values do not cause an attitudinal change.

14. In coaching, decisions have to be consensual.

15. Relationship is the foundation of coaching.

16. Successful leadership requires one to determine personal information about each supervised officer.

17. Communication is an art and skill that can be learned.

18. Nonverbal cues can assess the true meaning of the content of a message.

19. A good listener tunes out dry subjects.

20. An effective listener must be flexible.

21. A poor listener interprets color and emotional words.

22. A good listener mentally summarizes.

23. A poor listener listens for facts.

24. The most effective coaching process involves one-way communication.

25. Active listening is the most ineffective listening technique.

26. It is easy to disguise a lack of human skills.

27. First-line supervisors are an agency's quality-control agents.

28. Feedback is a compelling coaching skill.

29. Feedback must be in writing.

30. Constructive feedback can be of three types.

31. Constructive feedback can be based on opinions.

32. Every officer needs to be coaxed constantly.

33. Very few officers have the ability to change from low to high commitment.

34. Developmental counseling is supervisor-centered.

35. Intention is a feature of a successful style.

36. The intention of counseling is not punitive in nature.

37. There are five styles of counseling.

38. Nondirective counseling encourages maturity.

39. Mentoring is an old concept in law enforcement.

CHAPTER 10 Discipline—An Essential Element of Police Supervision

LEARNING OBJECTIVES

1. Define discipline.
2. Compare and contrast the various forms of discipline.
3. Identify the characteristics of an effective disciplinary system.
4. Describe the role of and skills needed by first-line supervisors.
5. Explore the use and abuse of disciplinary action in complex organizations.
6. Understand the keys to effective discipline.
7. Identify the types of disciplinary action available to the first-line supervisor.
8. Identify the five reaction stages for an individual going through disciplinary action.
9. Develop an appreciation for "firm but fair" disciplinary action.
10. Understand discipline as a multidimensional learning process.

KEY TERMS

- "hot stove" concept
- bill of rights
- constructive discharge
- constructive discipline
- progressive discipline
- disciplinary action
- disciplinary action made to stick
- firm, fair, equitable, and lawful
- first-line supervisors as disciplinarians
- goal of discipline
- negative discipline
- objectives of the discipline system
- peace officer
- positive discipline
- PRICE protocol
- property right
- total quality management
- types of discipline
- vicarious liability

Chapter Summary

I Nature of Discipline

The goal of discipline is to produce desirable behavior. It is considered an essential element of work that ensures overall productivity and an orderly environment. Discipline has numerous meanings and uses, but it tends to have negative connotations for many people. In its best context, discipline is considered positive and involves teaching, instruction, training, and remediation. Its purpose is to facilitate corrective action, resulting in self-control that is based on the norms and values of the workforce, producing predictable behavior and organizational efficiency. From this perspective, discipline is a management function.

Sergeants are responsible for nurturing professionalism in officers, and they are also responsible for initiating disciplinary measures when formal action is required. First-line supervisors have to find a balance between self-regulation and organizational control in order to achieve the organization's mission and objectives.

II Positive Discipline

A. Positive Discipline. A systematic approach designed to instruct and/or guide employees, so that they become loyal, dedicated, responsible, and productive employees.

First-line supervisors should strive to create an environment in which self-discipline is rewarded and where imposed discipline is held to a minimum. Effective supervisors help keep subordinates interested in their jobs and satisfied with working conditions. They must be multidimensional, fulfilling a variety of roles, accentuating the positive, and cultivating employee self-worth. Money and other material rewards are very powerful, but recognition that is genuine can have an even greater impact on job-related behavior.

To be effective, a supervisor needs to develop the ability to criticize the work the employee does, and not the employee. Once certain parameters for accepted behavior are internalized, they serve as a basis for self-control. When employees learn the job and know the standards that they are judged on, they will gain a great deal of self-confidence and personal security.

Total Quality Management (TQM) empowers employees to create a positive, performance-oriented culture and employee commitment. First-line supervisors must be facilitators in this participative approach.

The authors state that a supervisor can guarantee an improvement in performance through the **PRICE protocol**, which is:

1. *Pinpoint.* Identify performance problems that must be addressed.

2. *Record.* Document the current performance level of those having problems.

3. *Involve.* Involve officers in determining the best way to deal with problems, the coaching strategies to be used, and how the supervisor will monitor the progress and the rewards or punishments that will occur based on the success or failure of the corrective process.

4. *Coach.* Carry out the agreed-upon coaching strategies by observing and offering timely advice, encouragement, positive reinforcement, and retraining.

5. *Evaluate.* Evaluate and provide feedback on a continuous basis to decide whether the goals of the PRICE protocol have been achieved.

III Negative Discipline

A. Negative Discipline. Discipline based on the use of punishment, rather than rewards.

In police organizations, supervisors spend a great deal of time and energy coping with marginal employees. When all else fails, sergeants are forced to rely on the imposition of negative discipline to deal with both deviant and marginal personnel. The sergeant must:

1. Identify weaknesses or deficiencies, failures, or overt behavior that require corrective action.

2. Analyze all the factors to assess appropriate action.

3. Initiate and possibly carry out the disciplinary action.

4. Document the case as to cause, analysis, action, and appropriateness.

Sergeants must act reasonably, decisively, and promptly to resolve discipline problems. They have to consider the needs of the employee, the department, the law enforcement profession, and the community. They should strive for **constructive discipline** that is **firm**, **fair**, and impartial. Discipline should not be applied randomly. Sergeants must recognize the needs of their subordinates in order to avoid job dissatisfaction, interpersonal conflicts, poor performance, discipline problems, and high turnover.

IV Disciplinary Systems

Good disciplinary systems do not come about by accident, but rather by being designed carefully by management. They include the following characteristics:

1. Proper assignment of personnel to a job according to their interest, skill, and training.

2. Necessary and reasonable job-related policies, procedures, rules, and regulations to meet employee needs and accomplish the department's goals and objectives.

3. Effective communication regarding performance and acceptable behavior along with explanations of consequences if not followed.

4. Continuous review, evaluation, and appraisal of personnel.

5. Consistent, fair, and **equitable** enforcement of all policies, procedures, rules, and regulations.

6. Mutually acceptable disciplinary procedures based on the "due process" model.

7. A formal appeals procedure designed to ensure fairness of all disciplinary actions and serve as a check and balance on the imposition of punitive sanctions.

Two distinct objectives of disciplinary actions are to (1) reform the individual offender and (2) deter others who may have been influenced by the incident. Sergeants must review which penalties are available, feasible, and appropriate in each circumstance. There is no place for anger, revenge, or retribution in the discipline process. It is illegal for a supervisor to misuse power or harass an employee.

The imposition of discipline without just cause is viewed as an unconscionable and unacceptable abuse of authority.

Effective disciplinarians are proactive as well as reactive. Good supervisors know the keys to effective discipline:

1. Do not be a discipline ostrich—do not overlook discipline problems.

2. Be a "Caesar's wife"—all of the sergeant's behavior should be above reproach.

3. Practice the "hot stove" rule—discipline should be immediate, based on known rules, consistent, and impersonal.

4. Never lose control.

5. Be instructive.

6. Be firm, but fair.

7. Stay out of the employee's private life.

8. State rules/regulations in a positive manner.

9. Do not be a disciplinary magician—do not make up rules as you go along.

10. Be precise—comply with labor laws, collective bargaining agreements, and civil service regulations. Follow procedures and document actions.

Good supervisors also understand that individuals involved in a disciplinary action may react with denial, anger, by bargaining, depression, and acceptance. A good supervisor allows the officer to experience and progress through each of the reaction stages.

V The Hot Stove Concept

Douglas McGregor compared an organization's disciplinary system to a red-hot stove. When you touch a red-hot stove, the discipline is immediate, predictable, consistent, and totally impersonal. Under McGregor's theory, the stove not only serves as a deterrent against whom it is applied, but will also train other employees about what the organization will not accept. Telling employees what is expected of them and explaining the negative consequences they may face is an absolute requirement for effective discipline in law enforcement.

VI Disciplinary Action

Sergeants play a key role in the police discipline system and have tremendous influence on the process. Firm and fair discipline depends on four critical factors:

1. Quality of the personnel being recruited by the department.
2. Effectiveness of the promotion system.
3. Training given to newly promoted sergeants.
4. Support that first-line supervisors receive from their superiors.

The decision to use discipline should be made with care. Most departments use a **progressive discipline** system that provides for increases in punishment for each subsequent offense:

1. Informal discussion.
2. Oral warning.
3. Written reprimand.

4. Final written warning.
5. Suspension.
6. Demotion.
7. Discharge.

Progressive discipline uses the belief that the punishment should fit the crime. However, it is not the answer to every problem. It is merely a tool. It will not work with some employee personalities. If the decision to fire an employee is made, it will be accomplished through the progressive discipline system. The goal of discipline is to redirect an employee's negative behavior and salvage the employee.

Discipline can be used to promote efficiency and increase job productivity. How the supervisor carries it out will determine the liability the department will incur if the discipline is challenged as unfair labor practice.

VII *Making Disciplinary Action Stick*

Disciplinary action can be a tool to promote efficiency, effectiveness, and productivity. Reasonable disciplinary action can be made to stick if it is fair and if first-line supervisors learn to avoid certain mistakes:

1. No specific offense or violation of policy determined.
2. Insufficient warning that the employee's performance or misconduct is unacceptable.
3. No positive evidence to support the charges against the employee.
4. Supervisor demonstrates real or perceived favoritism or discrimination toward employees.
5. No documentation kept of warnings or reprimands.
6. Punishment is severe or excessive.
7. No concern for just cause and procedural due process.

When discipline is not maintained within a department or treated indifferently by supervisors or managers, the quality of service delivered to the community is lowered and the integrity of the profession suffers.

Employers and supervisors can be subject to civil action in the form of monetary and/or injunctive relief if it is found that the department has fallen short in certain obligations:

1. Negligent or wrongful acts of employees.
2. Failure to train.

3. Failure to supervise.
4. Failure to discipline.

Multiple-Choice Questions (Circle the Best Answer)

1. Discipline is
   a. an adversarial process.
   b. a tool for achieving shared purpose and goal-oriented behavior.
   c. a means of teaching, training, and remediation.
   d. all of the above.

2. Every first-line supervisor should strive to create an environment in which
   a. sanctions are relied on for results.
   b. external or imposed discipline is held to an absolute minimum.
   c. an employee's sense of competence, craftsmanship, and pride is cultivated through discipline.
   d. none of the above.

3. _____ are among the most powerful motivators at the disposal of the first-line supervisor.
   a. Disciplinary actions
   b. Shift assignments
   c. Commendations and citations

4. _____ are two of the things mentioned in the text that create natural parameters for accepted and expected behavior in a given organization.
   a. Rules and regulations
   b. Effective supervision and discipline
   c. Technical expertise and discipline
   d. Camaraderie and technical expertise

5. According to More and Miller, _____ and _____ come with the stripes.

    a. power, authority

    b. respect, power

    c. problem solving, counseling

    d. power, discipline

6. Police officers have emotional job-related security needs, including all of the following except

    a. the need to know exactly what management expects as to work performance and conduct.

    b. the need for regular feedback from management concerning job performance.

    c. the need to be treated fairly and impartially by those in management.

    d. none of the above.

7. According to Peters and Waterman, based on the "people orientation" of contemporary management theory, there is no place for _____ in the disciplinary process.

    a. friendship

    b. guilt

    c. anger

    d. reform

8. The misuse of power by the first-line supervisor does all but which of the following?

    a. Destroys the sergeant's credibility.

    b. Enhances legitimate authority over subordinates.

    c. Undermines the sergeant's effectiveness.

    d. Subjects management to ridicule, charges of unfair labor practices, political repercussions, and civil suits.

9. Disciplinary action should be

    a. proactive.

    b. reactive.

    c. both proactive and reactive.

10. According to the hot stove rule, employees learn quickly because discipline is all but which of the following?

    a. Immediate.

    b. Predictable.

    c. Consistent.

    d. Personal.

11. Whether the discipline is firm and fair will depend on critical factors that include all but which of the following?

    a. Quality of the personnel being recruited by the department.

    b. Accountability of the management system.

    c. Training given to newly promoted sergeants.

    d. Support that first-line supervisors receive from their superiors.

12. Effective disciplinary action is always

    a. based on just cause.

    b. appropriate to the offense and the needs of the offender.

    c. progressively more severe if the subordinate fails to change errant, disruptive, or deviant behavior.

    d. all of the above.

13. Discipline based on the use of punishment rather than rewards is

    a. positive discipline.

    b. negative discipline.

    c. retributive discipline.

    d. penal discipline.

True or False Questions

1. Discipline is the essential element in work that ensures overall productivity and an orderly environment.

2. Discipline may be used to produce a shared sense of purpose and common goal-oriented behavior.

3. First-line supervisors are expected to nurture professionalism in the employee.

4. According to More and Miller, the first-line supervisor will determine the success or failure of the police department in achieving its mission, goals, and objectives.

5. According to O.W. Wilson, positive discipline manifests itself in the officer's willingness to conform and participate in self-restraint based on professional dedication or a personal commitment to the ethos of the police department.

6. Disciplinary action is inherently punitive and used to regulate work-related behavior.

7. Sergeants are expected to increase the employee's productivity through negative discipline.

8. It is the first-line supervisor's responsibility to identify the weaknesses, deficiencies, failure, or overt behavior of subordinates.

9. Inconsistency and favoritism in disciplining subordinates will have an adverse, potentially destructive effect on employee productivity.

10. A sergeant's actions must be legal, reasonable, inconsistent, and timely.

11. If a sergeant misunderstands the nature of the job or lacks rudimentary leadership skills, the potential for abuse of the disciplinary apparatus is great.

12. The accused employee is presumed innocent until proven guilty, and the burden of proof is on those involved in direct supervisory management.

13. First-line supervisors have a duty to act in the best interests of all of the following: the employee, the department, the law enforcement profession, and the community at large.

14. Supervisory personnel who bend or break the rules promote disruptive and deviant behavior by others in the workforce.

15. One key to success as a disciplinarian is to ensure that all employees know and fully understand the department's policies, procedures, rules, and regulations.

16. Failure to sustain a disciplinary action against an employee puts the supervisor at risk for a subsequent civil suit.

17. When a subject going through the process of a disciplinary action exhibits anger or disrespectful behavior, immediate suspension should occur.

18. According to the authors, the two primary objectives of disciplinary actions are to (1) create loyalty to the department and (2) instill respect for authority.

CHAPTER 11 Internal Discipline—A System of Accountability

LEARNING OBJECTIVES

1. Identify and describe several forms of police deviance.
2. Explore the basic concept of administrative responsibility.
3. Discuss the need for a formal internal investigation policy.
4. Examine the synergistic balance of factors required to keep police misconduct under control.
5. Differentiate between the sources of personnel complaints.
6. Identify the three major types of police misconduct complaints.
7. Describe, compare, and contrast the four phases of the internal discipline process.
8. List the steps involved in a police personnel investigation.
9. Examine the structure and function of a police trial board.
10. Develop an appreciation for the importance of procedural due process.
11. Understand how complaint dispositions should be classified.
12. Explore the various roles played by the sergeant in the administration of internal discipline.
13. Discuss the role of the chief police executive in providing leadership for and control of the disciplinary system.
14. Examine the relationship among the early warning system, the employee assistance program, and total quality management of police personnel.

KEY TERMS

- adjudication
- complaint receipt
- disciplinary action
- dispositions
- due process
- early warning system
- employee assistance programs
- executive leadership
- fairness
- internal discipline
- occupational deviance
- participation
- personnel complaints
- police deviance
- police misconduct
- proactive policy
- professionalism
- responsibility
- supervisor's role
- trial boards

Chapter Summary

I Police Work

Police work has become highly complex, with a majority of an officer's time spent keeping the peace and providing nonpolice services. Even though it can be rewarding, police work is often also unappreciated and unpleasant. Due to broad discretionary power, the complexity of their work, and some of the people that the work requires officers to come into contact with, police are particularly vulnerable to corruption and deviance.

A. **Police Deviance.** Activities inconsistent with an officer's legal authority, organizational authority, or standards of ethical conduct.

B. **Corruption.** Refers to the sale of legitimate authority for personal gain. **Occupational deviance** has been classified into three categories:

1. *Nonfeasance.* Failure to take appropriate action as required by law or department policy.

2. *Misfeasance.* Performing a required and lawful task in an unacceptable, inappropriate, or unprofessional manner.

3. *Malfeasance.* Wrongdoing or illegal conduct dependent on or related to the misuse of legitimate authority.

Occupational deviance includes the following:

1. Corruption.
2. Unlawful use of force.
3. Mistreatment of prisoners.
4. Discrimination.
5. Illegal search and seizure.
6. Perjury.
7. Planting of evidence.
8. Other misconduct committed under the color of police authority.

Researchers have identified five problem areas in urban policing, which can be considered institutional preconditions for crime, corruption, and deviance:

1. Wide discretion.
2. Low managerial visibility.

3. Low public visibility.
4. Peer group secrecy.
5. Managerial secrecy.

The most effective way to fight deviance and corruption is to build a strong supervisory structure. Sergeants must be empowered with the authority and the training to control the behavior of subordinates. First-line supervisors must make a proactive commitment to integrity.

Each officer must be consistently held accountable for poor on-the-job performance or inappropriate behavior. Management must set down realistic ethical and professional standards for supervisors to use to judge employees.

Police officers have a difficult time shedding the "superhero" image that comes from public perceptions. To maintain the respect and integrity of the department, management needs to have a strong system of continuous monitoring for accountability and **internal discipline**. This is not an easy task for management, as it will require:

1. Revising inadequate policies and procedures.
2. Correcting or separating from police service those who are found guilty of serious professional misconduct.

II Controlling the Police

The concept of **responsibility** includes professional ethics, answerability, and accountability. Because the police are key to safeguarding the democratic process, occupational deviance cannot be tolerated. These three ingredients are essential to police **professionalism** and have been incorporated into a new police code of conduct. It is management's role and responsibility to develop and implement the policies, procedures, rules, and regulations needed to take the ethics theory and turn it into practice. First-line supervisors must play an important part in making sure this internal discipline works properly. The chief executive officer is responsible for the discipline and control of all subordinate personnel. Policing the police is imperative to gain or hold the respect of the community. This trust and respect from the community prevent civil unrest from erupting.

III Personnel Complaint Investigation Policy

If the department implements a strong policy that clearly defines, prohibits, and encourages the reporting of occupational deviance, it is a giant step toward accountability. The control of discretion is essential.

Police managers should proactively seek out deviant behavior and investigate the substantive complaints made against officers. However, police officers must fully understand the regulations if they are to follow them. Policy must be written, so that it is clear and not over-rigid, yet it must strike a synergistic balance among managerial control, community expectations, professional ethics, and discretionary flexibility (Figure 11.1). Procedures for investigating personnel will vary depending on the origin, nature, and seriousness of the allegation. The text lists seven basic steps of a more structured and formal procedure needed for serious complaints.

IV Personnel Complaints

A. Personnel Complaint. A formal accusation alleging that a specific employee is guilty of legal, moral, or professional misconduct.

Trivial complaints should be filtered out immediately and disposed of through proper administrative action. Complaints that have substance should be moved into the internal investigation process.

1. *Internal complaint.* A complaint that originates from within the department. These types of complaints are initiated by first-line supervisors or command-level officers who have witnessed occupational deviance. These complaints may also come from fellow officers who know about or strongly suspect misconduct.

2. *External complaints.* Come from outside the department such as from lawyers, pressure groups, elected officials, relatives, and others who have chosen to focus on **police misconduct**.

A first-line supervisor must be concerned about the **due process**. The supervisor must determine whether a complaint is legitimate and accurate. Complaints offer supervisors and management excellent feedback by increasing awareness of potential problem areas. Legitimate complaints should not be discouraged, as they support the department's commitment to police their own.

There are three types of complaints:

1. *Primary complaint.* Received directly from the victim.

2. *Secondary complaint.* Received from persons who are not the victims, but who are complaining on behalf of others.

3. *Anonymous.* Complaints of occupational deviance from an unidentified source. Anonymous complaints should be handled with the greatest care due to the possible impact on the morale of those involved. However, management cannot afford to dismiss these complaints simply because the source is unidentified.

V Social Media

Law enforcement agencies are increasingly implementing policies regarding employee use of social media. Many police agencies have been made aware of how social media affect their image in the community by the postings on Facebook, MySpace, and Twitter by police employees. Most law enforcement agencies have policies in place, which deal with how employees are to conduct themselves while off duty. In 2010, the International Association of Chiefs of Police (IACP) issued a model policy to guide police agencies in developing policies that deal with social media postings by officers. The model policy states that sworn and non-sworn police employees "should be mindful that their speech becomes part of the worldwide electronic domain" (International Association of Chiefs of Police, 2010). The best recommendation is for police officers and supervisors to refrain from being friends with subordinates on social media sites and abstain from posting statements which may cast them and their departments in a bad light with the community.

VI Personnel Complaint Investigations

Because of the wide range in size and sophistication of the more than 18,000 law enforcement agencies in the United States, it is difficult to state the sergeant's typical role in personnel complaint investigations. However, because sergeants are often the most visible and approachable part of the management team, it is likely that most complaints of misconduct will be channeled through them.

Depending on their authority, sergeants monitor performance and serve as the department's mental disciplinarians. In minor cases involving police deviance, they may bring charges, investigate, adjudicate, and punish subordinates when appropriate—subject to administrative review and consistent with departmental policy, civil service regulations, collective bargaining agreements, and the law. Investigating alleged police misconduct requires a great deal of skill, and the person performing this task needs specific training, guidance, and support. Internal investigation procedures should be swift, certain, fair, and lawful.

Once a formal personnel complaint is placed into the internal investigation process, official fact-finding begins. The tools and techniques used to investigate police misconduct should not differ from those used in other types of investigations. The first step is to interview the complainant to gather information, identify witnesses and leads, assess the complainant's credibility, determine merits of the accusation, and ascertain any possible motives of the complainant. The investigator should be discreet and skillful in handling the complainant interview, being careful not to reveal information or prejudge the case. It is important to keep written records that are clear, concise, accurate, and factual.

First-line supervisors and other internal personnel complaint investigators should be familiar with administrative and constitutional rules governing the procedural due process, which protect officers who are not guilty and make sure that those who are guilty are treated fairly. Once the complainant interview reveals a need to proceed with an investigation, this investigation should be expedited. Delays hamper inquiry, reduce employee morale, and erode public confidence in the police force. After all relevant evidence has been gathered and evaluated, the investigating officer must try to determine a way to prove or disprove the allegation, and the findings should be included in a comprehensive investigation report that includes a recommendation for **disposition** of the case that is then forwarded to the appropriate person for action. Internal investigations should be concluded within 30 days.

Administrative procedure should not be a substitute for criminal prosecution when criminal misconduct is determined.

VII Adjudication

The chief administrator is responsible for determining the final disposition of all complaints. Personnel complaint dispositions are classified into one of the following:

1. Sustained indicates, based on the facts obtained, that the accused committed all or part of the alleged police misconduct.

2. Not sustained means that the investigation produced insufficient evidence to prove or disprove the allegation and that the matter is being resolved in favor of the employee.

3. Exonerated denotes that the alleged act or omission occurred, but was, in fact, legal, proper, and necessary.

4. Unfounded is used when the alleged police misconduct did not occur and the complaint was false.

5. Misconduct not based on original complaint means that while there was misconduct by the police officer, and it was separate and distinct from that alleged in the original complaint.

If the complaint was investigated by someone other than the first-line supervisor, the sergeant should be contacted before the final disposition is made. The sergeant's input should be evaluated carefully for objectivity and consistency; however, this is the best person to evaluate an officer's overall job performance, professional conduct, and value as an employee.

It is recommended by Nathan Iannone that the safest way to protect the department from civil liability in cases involving serious legal, moral, or professional misconduct is to follow the Supreme Court decision in Morrissey v. Brewer, which identifies the minimum requirements of the procedural due process to which officers are entitled.

Many police departments have developed some type of **trial board** system to help make decisions in internal discipline cases. These boards are administrative in nature and are meant to provide a "neutral and detached" body that is expected to use rational, objective, and analytical reasoning in reaching a decision.

Their role is strictly advisory. This board must be carefully monitored and managed to remain effective.

VIII Civilian Review Movement

This movement has resurrected itself and is based on the need for accountability of the police department. This group usually has no power to discipline, but it brings openness, raises issues of concern, and marshals public sentiment. Many officers and unions oppose outside review of any sort, and it is yet to be seen if civilian review boards will survive.

IX Forecasting

Forecasting potential employees prone to misconduct has become a popular management tool. The **early warning system** is structured to track complaints in order to flag potential problem employees and leads to a key interview with the employee. When appropriate, managers may recommend help in the form of coaching, counseling, professional care, or referral to an **employee assistance program** (EAP). The early warning system is diagnostic and help-oriented rather than punitive.

Based on the assumption that it is more humane and cost-effective to salvage an existing human resource, EAPs provide opportunities for intervention and remediation.

Multiple-Choice Questions (Circle the Best Answer)

1. _____, secrecy, and lack of supervision are three important factors leading to police deviance.

    a. Violence

    b. Ignorance

    c. Peer pressure

    d. Discretion

2. Responsibility encompasses professional ethics, answerability, and

    a. society's expectations.

    b. regulations.

    c. commitment.

    d. accountability.

3. The _____ is ultimately responsible for the discipline and control of all subordinate personnel.

    a. chief executive officer

    b. district attorney

    c. first-line supervisor

    d. precinct captain

4. Sergeants have a/an _____ obligation to accept and investigate all legitimate allegations of personal or professional misconduct.

    a. ethical and functional

    b. managerial and functional

    c. ethical and managerial

    d. lawful and functional

5. Performing a required and lawful task in an unacceptable, inappropriate, or unprofessional manner describes

    a. malfeasance.

    b. misfeasance.

    c. corruption.

    d. misconduct.

6. The internal affairs investigation process must be _____ and lawful.

    a. positive, swift, certain

    b. swift, certain, fair

c. positive, swift, formal

d. swift, fair, anonymous

7. The investigative effort expended on any internal discipline complaint should be at least equal to the effort expended in the investigation of a _____ crime, where a suspect is known.

   a. felony

   b. misdemeanor

8. The first step in a personnel investigation is to

   a. commit the police department to a particular course of action regarding the internal investigation.

   b. indicate personal professional opinion on the matter.

   c. prejudge the validity of the complainant.

   d. interview the complainant.

9. Personnel complaints filed anonymously should be

   a. discounted as invalid.

   b. handled with the greatest care and utmost discretion.

10. A police employee whose internal investigation complaint has been sustained should be allowed to appeal a chief executive's decision and the police agency should

    a. provide the resources for the appeal.

    b. provide the funds for the appeal.

    c. not provide the resources or the funds for the appeal.

11. Which of the following dispositions is added to the five-category system, giving the chief executive officer more latitude and flexibility?

    a. Sustained.

    b. Exonerated.

    c. Misconduct not based on original complaint.

d. Not sustained.

e. Unfounded.

12. When an internal discipline complaint is sustained, which of the following is used more frequently in serious misconduct cases?

    a. Reassignment.

    b. Loss of seniority.

    c. Psychological counseling.

    d. Participation in a multipurpose EAP.

13. Police officers who, because of alcohol or other drug abuse, cannot function temporarily should be

    a. suspended without pay immediately.

    b. taken home by the supervisor and dealt with later.

    c. arrested and booked.

    d. taken to the chief executive officer by the supervisor.

14. According to Nathan Iannone, almost any _____ order to an employee is enforceable administratively.

    a. lawful

    b. reasonable

    c. direct

    d. indirect

15. Iannone suggests that the safest way to avoid reversal and civil liability in internal discipline cases involving legal, moral, or professional misconduct is to adhere to the requirements outlined in

    a. Morrissey v. Brewer.

    b. Morrison v. Bakke.

    c. Morrow v. Brown.

    d. Morley v. Brooks.

16. The Supreme Court case mentioned in Question 15 outlines

    a. a new police code of conduct.

    b. minimum requirements of the procedural due process.

    c. legal obligations of the management.

    d. constitutional rights and obligations.

17. The renewed interest in civilian review boards is referred to as a/an _____ movement in the text.

    a. futile

    b. advocacy

    c. innovative

    d. accountability

18. According to More and Miller, ideally the administrative trial board should consist of _____ police officers from within the department.

    a. seven

    b. six

    c. five

    d. four

19. Trial board members are responsible for determining _____ and making a recommendation to the chief executive.

    a. innocence

    b. guilt

    c. fact

20. Decisions of the trial board should be based on

    a. proof beyond a reasonable doubt.

    b. a preponderance of the evidence.

21. According to the text, which city's trial board became so bad that the city had to seek state legislative relief to correct the problem?

    a. Los Angeles.

    b. Chicago.

    c. New York.

    d. Pittsburgh.

22. In an effort to minimize the need for formal disciplinary action in cases involving noncriminal and less serious police deviance, departments are experimenting with

    a. coaching and counseling.

    b. EAPs and early warning systems.

    c. retraining.

    d. extended probation.

True or False Questions

1. Police represent the fine line that separates freedom from chaos and legitimate social control from tyranny.

2. According to Mark Baker, police officers are a composite of their unique experiences and are different from the people they police.

3. Failure to take appropriate action as required by law or department policy is considered malfeasance.

4. Corruption deals with illegal acts.

5. Police administrators and civilian review boards are responsible for policing the police.

6. Researchers have identified seven basic problems in urban policing, which are regarded as institutional preconditions for police crime, corruption, and occupational deviance.

7. Supervisors and managers must make an upfront and proactive commitment to integrity.

8. Ethical ambiguity permits the police to operate in a vacuum.

9. The principal function of police is the safeguarding of the democratic process.

10. First-line supervisors are the operating engineers who make sure the internal discipline apparatus works properly.

11. Policy creates unrealistic parameters that control the use of discretion in complex criminal justice organizations.

12. It is no longer sufficient to only react to complaints initiated by those outside the organization.

13. The internal discipline system should be based on essential fairness and bound by formal procedures and proceedings, such as are used in criminal trials.

14. The control of discretion is absolutely essential if the department is to protect the accused employee from unfounded and/or malicious allegations of occupational deviance.

15. A police department's personnel complaint investigation policy should be written to cover every possible contingency to protect the accused employee and the department.

16. The written personnel complaint investigation policy statement must be crafted carefully to strike a simplistic balance between managerial control and officers' expectations.

17. Misconduct complaints lodged against police officers come from three sources.

18. According to Iannone, some of the most frivolous complaints about police misconduct have been brought to light by anonymous information.

19. Supervisors need to be cautious about limiting subordinates' use of social media.

CHAPTER 12 Supervising the Difficult Employee—Special Considerations

LEARNING OBJECTIVES

1. Describe a typical value statement for a police department.
2. List the five characteristics of a problem employee.
3. Compare an ascendant employee with an ambivalent employee.
4. Identify the characteristics of an erudite employee.
5. Describe the type of employee who can be classified as a manipulator.
6. List the five types of problem employees.
7. Identify the view taken by most marginal employees.
8. Write a short essay describing work stressors.
9. List the six task stressors.
10. Describe the nature and extent of suicide in law enforcement.
11. Identify the key elements of an early warning system.
12. Describe the types of problems that can be dealt with by an employee assistance program.

KEY TERMS

- alcohol
- ambivalent employees
- ascendant employees
- critical incident stress management
- defeatists
- departmental values
- divorce
- early warning systems
- employee assistance program
- erudites
- indecisives
- indifferent employees
- manipulators
- marginal performers
- millennials
- peer counseling
- post-traumatic stress disorder
- problem employees
- suicide
- task stressors
- tyrants
- value statements work stressors

Chapter Summary

Today's supervisors must set the tone and lay a foundation for a strong and supportive work environment. **Value statements** set the tone for many organizations, representing ideals that serve as the foundation for policies, goals, and operations. They are reminders of the factors that contribute to a positive work environment.

I *Types of Employees*

While it is not easy to categorize employees, organizations generally consist of three types of individuals. Employees must be viewed on an individual basis, but these generalized groups help in viewing conduct similar to other employees.

A. **Ascendant.** These employees are work-oriented, success-driven, and highly focused on their assignments. They are highly self-confident and like challenging assignments. They thrive on recognition and promotion. They are loners who generally think they are the only ones to accomplish tasks well. The negative side of this employee is that they are intolerant of other employees who do not work to their standards. Tasks will usually be done correctly and efficiently, with little need for supervision. Their allegiance is to the profession rather than the department.

B. **Indifferent.** These employees perform duties at an acceptable, minimal level. Their concentration is on getting by, and their focus is usually on family or nondepartmental activities. They do just enough to get by and avoid discipline, resisting any change. They are highly social with other officers and tend to strengthen informal work groups. They are difficult to supervise because motivational efforts have a short span, and they require close supervision.

C. **Ambivalent.** These officers are creative and intelligent. They will seek out critical areas of the job and gather knowledge about them. However, routine work becomes stagnant and boring, and they become procrastinators. As the frustration level increases, these officers become less decisive and resist any procedural changes. This employee may or may not seek upward mobility. However, if these employees receive challenging tasks, they are hardworking. They enjoy rewards and praise.

Supervisor expectations are critical to subordinate performance, and acceptable levels of job performance should be made clear to all employees. Setting high standards is necessary in order to achieve high performance.

II Problem Employees

Supervisors spend a great deal of time dealing with conflict and problem employees. Problem situations must be dealt with before they have a negative impact on other employees and the organization itself.

A. **Erudites.** These employees always have an opinion and see themselves as intellectuals. They show a low tolerance of other people; however, they will follow departmental procedures. They will try to use their expertise to influence decisions. First-line supervisors need to guard against allowing them to take over as a leader.

B. **Tyrants.** These employees are control-oriented and fail to respect others. They will show explosive outbursts and work at intimidating people. They want to control the situation and must win at all costs, even if they have to resort to coercion or fear. The supervisor must react to this employee by responding at the same level to maintain control and stop the employee's aggressive behavior. Any confrontation should be done privately and as often as necessary.

C. **Defeatists.** These employees are chronic complainers and resist every new idea. The first-line supervisor must force this employee to deal with specifics rather than generalizations. The first-line supervisor must confront this employee and make the employee explain his or her position, clarifying the situation and dealing with the specific problem.

D. **Manipulators.** These employees are unethical, thriving on half-truths and innuendo. They gather knowledge to build power. They focus on dividing and conquering and will pit one person against the other. If they can create enough conflict and confusion, they can manipulate others more effectively. The first-line supervisor must investigate each action taken by this person and then form an opinion based on facts to refute the manipulator objectively.

E. **Indecisives.** These employees do not like to make decisions and will avoid doing so at all costs. They rarely express their attitudes and beliefs and are expert procrastinators. They believe that if they do not give an opinion, they cannot be judged. The first-line supervisor should try to identify why these employees refuse to make decisions. This is best affected by direct questioning to clarify areas of confusion and then requiring the officer to respond clearly about the problem. The supervisor should not settle for anything less than a direct answer.

III Marginal Performers

Marginal performers do just enough to get by. They perform tasks more slowly than normal and take advantage of things that benefit them directly, such as meal breaks and coffee breaks. They are usually late and will abuse sick time. They will work at giving themselves the appearance that they are working harder; however, it will be nonproductive work. Their complacency affects everything about their job, and their priorities are outside of their job. They are generally passive, not goal-oriented, and do not accept responsibility for their lack of productivity. They simply blame management.

The first-line supervisor should set down goals for these employees, making sure to provide a plan to reach those goals. These employees need to understand their place within the organization and what makes up a working relationship. However, they need to receive praise and recognition for accomplishing tasks at an acceptable level. Timely positive reinforcement is important. The supervisor should have a positive attitude when dealing with these employees. However, if the employee fails to perform up to standards, the supervisor must document and take corrective action.

IV *Work Stressors*

Employees are affected by both organizational and personal stress. Stress can have a negative or a positive effect. However, the supervisor should focus concern on the negative effects of the stress, which can affect an officer's ability to work. Stress can show its effects through low productivity, abuse of sick leave, and low morale. Over time, stress can lead to a variety of illnesses and mental and personal problems that can affect an officer's productivity, health, and happiness—and can even be life-threatening.

I. **A. Task Stressors.** Stress that can affect the officer's work and personal life adversely. The main stressors identified are as follows:

1. Danger.

2. Boredom.

3. Role conflict and ambiguity.

4. Control over work.

5. Shift work.

6. Use of excessive force.

V *Personal Problems*

Because of the close working relationship with officers, the first-line supervisor may receive information, or officers may confide in the supervisor concerning personal stress. The supervisor may be able to help, or he or she may need to refer officers to an **employee assistance program** (EAP). Important problem areas include the following:

1. Suicide.

2. Alcohol abuse.

3. Divorce.

4. Spousal concerns about danger.

VI Early Warning System

Many agencies have instituted the "early warning system," which monitors officers' conduct and alerts management to inappropriate behavior. The system is nondisciplinary in nature. Behavioral activities are monitored, and officers at risk are identified for intervention. Responses might include counseling, training, referral to programs, psychological exams, physical exams, urinalysis, and so on. Problems identified through this system are frequently resolved through EAPs.

VII Employee Assistance Program

An EAP is a comprehensive program that may use in-house and/or external specialists. EAPs cover a wide range of services to help employees deal with emotional, family, psychological, financial, and retirement matters. Specialists work with the employee to get him or her back into the work environment and salvage the employee if possible.

VIII Critical Incident Stress Management

A. **Post-Traumatic Stress Disorder (PTSD).** A psychological condition caused by one's inability to successfully manage an emotional response triggered by severe trauma. PTSD has some typical symptoms that may serve as indicators. Early intervention after a critical incident can help eliminate the chance of the response developing into PTSD. It is very important that employees be debriefed after an incident.

B. **Peer Counseling.** A program that has been shown to be successful because officers often do not want to admit they have a stress-related problems; peer counselors are viewed as equals, and thus are more likely to be trusted by fellow officers. Peer counselors should receive extensive training before attempting to deal with these serious problems. However, peer counselors have been highly successful in dealing with problems such as alcoholism, drug abuse, terminal illness, deaths, on-the-job injuries, and retirement.

Multiple-Choice Questions (Circle the Best Answer)

1. What are the three types of individuals in an organization?

   a. Ascendant, indecisive, ambivalent.

   b. Ascendant, indifferent, and ambivalent.

   c. Manipulators, tyrants, and indecisives.

   d. Ambitious, indecisive, and marginal.

2. According to the text, the fundamental reasons officers commit suicide include all but which of the following?

   a. Despondency.

   b. Substance abuse.

   c. Personal problems.

   d. Any of the above.

3. For the marginal performer, which of the following is not correct?

   a. Never volunteer for any assignment.

   b. Primary interest is the department.

   c. Promotions are of little consequence.

   d. Top brass is viewed as being out of step with reality.

4. The supervisor, when dealing with a marginal employee, should strive to deal with the employee on a/an

   a. negative level.

   b. equal level.

   c. positive level.

   d. The supervisor should not deal with this employee, as the employee would view this as a weakness of the supervisor.

5. Organizational effects of work stressors include

   a. violence.

   b. marital problems.

c. accidents.

d. irresponsibility.

6. Personal effects of work stressors include

    a. increased errors.

    b. unpreparedness.

    c. irresponsibility.

    d. absenteeism.

7. _____ are the basis for beliefs and actions taken by a department.

    a. Foundations

    b. Policies

    c. Systems

    d. Values

8. _____ are two significant sources of stress for officers and the police organization, especially with the move toward community policing and an emphasis on solving community problems.

    a. Ambiguity and confusion

    b. Danger and workload

    c. Role conflict and ambiguity

    d. Budget and personnel

9. Evidence suggests that workload is not as critical to the health of a worker as the

    a. control the worker has over work pace.

    b. elimination of shift work.

    c. alleviation of boredom.

10. Which of the following attitudes is not representative of the ambivalent employee?

    a. Seeks approval and recognition.

b. Does not like to make decisions.

c. Reluctant to accept change.

d. Creative and intelligent.

11. The average day-shift worker gets _____ more hours of sleep weekly than the typical night-shift worker.

   a. 15

   b. 12

   c. 8

   d. 4

12. Researchers have suggested that civilian deaths caused by police are probably underreported by _____ percent.

   a. 50

   b. 30

   c. 20

   d. 5

13. In 2018, there were more than _____ assaults on officers.

   a. 61,000

   b. 71,000

   c. 58,866

   d. 91,000

14. According to Geller and Scott, all but which of the following are factors used to assess an officer's propensity to misuse force?

   a. Assignments, including partners and supervisors.

   b. Incidents resulting in injury.

   c. Absenteeism.

   d. Commendations and evaluations.

15. This employee type is seldom at a loss for words, viewing himself or herself as an intellectual in a class by himself or herself.

    a. Erudite.

    b. Manipulator.

    c. Expounder.

    d. Educated.

16. This officer type is difficult to judge because he or she hides his or her attitudes and beliefs, remaining as neutral as possible.

    a. Defeatist.

    b. Procrastinator.

    c. Ambivalent.

    d. Indecisive.

17. Most officers in an organization are _____; they are imaginative and intelligent, but bored easily by routine tasks, leading them to become procrastinators.

    a. ascendant

    b. ambivalent

    c. ambitious

    d. active

18. Problem employees are typically at what point in their careers?

    a. Rookie officers having a difficult time adapting are the most problematic.

    b. After about five years on the job, employees become frustrated with the sameness of their day-to-day routine, leading to problem behavior.

    c. Officers biding their time to retirement—who are past promotion opportunities and wanting to avoid dangerous situations—become problem employees.

    d. Inappropriate behavior can occur at any stage of an officer's employment, from newly appointed to retirement age.

True or False Questions

1. Supervisors are not required to change values and beliefs in efforts to set the tone, change the paradigms, and create foundations that result in a supportive work environment.

2. The first-line supervisor is the key if the changing organization is to become a learning organization.

3. Employees are responsible for results when they are part of the decision-making process.

4. Values are the basis for the beliefs and actions taken by a department.

5. According to More and Miller, "Each officer is a distinct person with a team player personality."

6. An ascendant officer is imaginative, intelligent, and spends considerable time becoming knowledgeable about critical areas.

7. Ambivalent employees perform their duties at what they perceive as an acceptable level, which proves to be minimal.

8. Indifferent employees seek promotions actively.

9. When conflict is created by officers, the supervisor has to spend a considerable amount of time dealing with the conflict.

10. Performance problems require a supervisor to analyze the situation carefully, give advice, and, if necessary, order the officer to resolve the problem.

11. Problem behavior evolves from a personality conflict between a supervisor and an officer.

12. Specific task stressors in law enforcement are usually not wide-ranging, but they do include role conflict and ambiguity.

13. EAPs offer the same type of assistance given to those who have a physical illness.

14. The quality of a psychological work environment should be such that employees learn their role and have a desire to please their immediate supervisor.

15. Marginal performers commit acts of commission as well as omission.

16. Police are three times more likely to commit suicide than be killed in the line of duty.

CHAPTER 13 Supervising Minorities— Respecting Individual and Cultural Differences

LEARNING OBJECTIVES

1. Explore white male dominance of police work in the United States.
2. Define de jure discrimination and contrast it with de facto discrimination.
3. Discuss and show the relationship among prejudice, stereotypes, and discrimination.
4. Examine Title VII and the Civil Rights Act of 1964 and the Equal Employment Opportunity Act in terms of their impact on equal employment opportunity in police work.
5. Identify the elements in affirmative action planning and explain the difference between a goal and a quota.
6. Describe the characteristics of a nondiscriminatory personnel selection process.
7. Understand how Equal Employment Opportunity Act/Affirmative Action has changed the composition of the workforce and implications for the future.
8. Discuss the importance of the sergeant's role in translating equal opportunity theory into practice.
9. List and discuss the traits that distinguish a promoted patrol officer from a competent supervisor when dealing with nontraditional police employees.
10. Discuss specific ways that a good first-line supervisor interacts with nontraditional employees in an effort to help develop their full potential.
11. Examine the components of the OUCH test and demonstrate its utility when it comes to supervising minorities.
12. Discuss the composition of protected classes based on the Civil Rights Act.
13. Explore the California approach to field training for first-line supervisors.

KEY TERMS

- affirmative action
- bona fide occupational qualification
- changing demographics
- Civil Rights Act of 1964
- competent and supportive supervisors
- dealing with sexual harassment
- discrimination
- Equal Employment Opportunity Act
- first-line supervisor's role
- managing a more educated workforce
- nondiscriminatory selection process
- nondiscriminatory supervisors
- OUCH test applied to supervision
- prejudice
- protected classes
- sexual diversity in the workforce
- strategies for supervising minorities
- supervising nontraditional employees
- training supervisors to do their job
- white male domination of police work

Chapter Summary

1 Coming to Grips with the Past

Until fairly recently, police departments were made up almost exclusively of politically conservative white males, primarily from the working class with a high school education and perhaps some military experience. Officers were hired to maintain the status quo. Police work and the composition of police departments have been undergoing gradual changes. However, police had often successfully used their political power to protect their turf when it came to minority hiring. It is crucial for departments to hire women and minorities in order to police their communities effectively. Participants in the criminal justice system must reflect the character of the community served.

Discrimination based on sex and race is a continuing problem in our society. Researcher Gary Johns believes that prejudgment based on previously acquired knowledge and past experience is normal. However, irrational categorization can stem from prejudgment in several forms:

1. *Prejudice.* A negative attitude toward a group of people considered different or inferior, based on observation and on ignorance, ethnocentrism, and xenophobia. Generalizations are applied to all members of a group despite individual differences.

2. *Stereotype.* A set of group-shared and generally negative attitudes based on tradition, limited interaction, or ignorance, which assigns similar undesirable attributes to all members of the out group.

3. *Discrimination.* This refers to the negative and unfavorable treatment of people based on their membership in a minority group. It can involve acts or omissions that affect the group negatively in order to satisfy a prejudice.

Prejudice, stereotyping, and discrimination are usually byproducts of uncontrolled ethnocentrism or xenophobia.

1. *Ethnocentrism.* The natural tendency of human beings to view their own culture and customs as right and superior, and to judge all others by those standards.

2. *Xenophobia.* The irrational fear or hatred of strangers and other foreigners. Minorities are often considered strangers in their own land.

Minority group. A part of the population that differs from others in some characteristics and is often subjected to differential treatment.

The **Civil Rights Act of 1964** prohibited discrimination based on national origin, ethnic group, sex, creed, age, or race. Title VII of the Act prohibits employers and unions from discriminating against employees in 15 areas. In 1966, the Equal Employment Opportunity Commission (EEOC) was created under authority of Title VII as a regulatory agency and was authorized to set standards and establish guidelines for compliance with the act. The **Equal Employment Opportunity Act** of 1972 extended coverage of Title VII to all state and local governments with more than 15 employees and gave the EEOC more authority to formulate policies, procedures, rules, and regulations designed to ensure compliance with the law.

Because these changes were not affecting a dramatic shift in the makeup of public service and nontraditional employees were not making it into higher ranks, the EEOC adopted a positive *affirmative action* policy. These guidelines were designed to promote activism without creating "reverse discrimination." The process involved four steps:

1. Analysis of major job categories to determine whether minorities were being underutilized.

2. Development of goals, timetables, and affirmative actions to correct deficiencies.

3. Maintenance of a database to determine if goals were being accomplished.

4. Constant assessment to prevent the reintroduction of discriminatory practices.

However, the concept of quotas and preferential treatment based on race, color, national origin, and sex is contrary to the law. Because most police departments use testing in the hiring process, the Supreme Court ruled in Griggs v. Duke Power Company that screening tests must be:

1. Valid.

2. Reliable.

3. Job-related.

4. Based on bona fide occupational qualification.

This decision was meant to protect candidates from arbitrary and discriminatory screening. Some police departments have moved away from comprehensive written tests and use assessment centers, which use multiple assessment strategies that involve various techniques to screen candidates, and have proven to be less discriminatory than other pre-employment screening procedures. However, this method requires a great deal of skill and is more costly.

II Changing Demographics

Clearly, women and minorities remain underrepresented at all levels, despite aggressive equal opportunity and affirmative action programs. Police managers should strive to comply with the National Advisory Commission on Criminal Justice Standards and Goals, Standard 13.3.

Managers, including sergeants, must ensure that discrimination is not a factor in hiring and that nothing is in place to prohibit minority officers from getting or holding jobs. The employment of minorities should be a recruiting goal rather than a quota governing hiring, and the composition of the community should be the guide when recruiting.

Recruitment. A multidimensional process designed to encourage people to seek careers in police work and to seek individuals qualified to do the job.

III Supervising Minorities

First-line supervisors are key to minority workers' success or failure. They must create an environment where all employees can satisfy needs while they work together to meet the goals and objectives of the department. Effective supervisors will be sensitive to individual differences and cultural differences among employees. Supervisors should:

1. Be knowledgeable, approachable, and empathetic.
2. Learn to listen and understand an employee's point of view.
3. Communicate openly and honestly.
4. Expect minorities to "test" the department's philosophy on human relations and the supervisor's commitment to equal employment opportunity.
5. Practice introspection and be aware of personal attitudes.

Supervisors should put together a plan to motivate employees. This plan should include the following:

1. Make the work interesting.
2. Relate rewards to performance.
3. Provide valued rewards.
4. Treat employees as individuals.
5. Encourage participation and cooperation.
6. Explain why the action is being taken.
7. Provide accurate and timely feedback.

Minority police officers are subjected not only to the normal stressors of police work, but also to the additional stress of skepticism and rejection by fellow officers, as well as not being fully accepted into the police culture. Female officers are subjected to additional and unique stressors:

1. Personal feelings of competence.
2. Perceptions of peers' view of competence.
3. Reluctant acceptance into the male-dominated police culture.
4. Unfavorable stereotypical reaction from citizens.
5. Sexual harassment.

Supervisors need to be extremely supportive of these officers. They should be firm, fair, and impartial. Sergeants are "change agents" who must work to rise above being merely promoted patrol officers. Managers must make a strong commitment to equal employment opportunities. The chief must set the stage and endorse a total no-nonsense policy to support equal employment opportunities, including continuous reinforcement.

IV Dealing with Employees in a Protected Class

a. **Protected Class.** A group of individuals who have been discriminated against unfairly or illegally in the past, or who are believed to be entitled to preferential consideration due to aspects of their life situation. This term is currently used as a classification based on employees' racial or ethnic origin, sex (gender or preference), age, physical status, and religion. A first-line supervisor should become very aware of those people who have minority status.

The OUCH test is probably the most informative for all actions of the supervisor:

Objective

Uniform in application

Consistently applied

Have job relatedness.

The OUCH test is recognized as a standard used by management and/or courts to determine whether real discrimination has occurred.

V Handling Sexual Harassment in the Workplace

Sexual harassment can take one of the two forms.

a. **Quid Pro Quo Sexual Harassment.** An individual is forced to grant sexual favors in order to obtain, maintain, or improve employment status.

b. **Hostile Work Environment Sexual Harassment.** Employees are subjected to suggestive comments, photographs, jokes, obscene gestures, or unwanted physical contact. The conduct has four elements: it (1) is unwelcome, (2) is sufficiently severe or pervasive to alter conditions of victim's employment and create an abusive environment, (3) is perceived by the victim as hostile or abusive, or (4) creates an environment that a reasonable person would find hostile or abusive.

Consistently, management has not been held liable for co-workers' sexual harassment. However, management must act in good faith, have a formal policy prohibiting sexual harassment, have a user-friendly and effective complaint procedure, and use appropriate disciplinary action in cases of sexual misconduct. The department can be held liable if a supervisor is in any way involved in harassment, and civil liability may arise if supervisors ignore harassment or fail to assist subordinates seeking a remedy. Supervisors need to help management spot, stop, and prevent sexual harassment.

VI Supervising Gay and Lesbian Police Officers

Sergeants must realize that they need to help in facilitating a change in human relations by welcoming diversity. Supervisors must clearly be open and accepting, demonstrating empathy in order to understand and utilize the talents of homosexual employees. Supervisors are change agents and culture carriers; they must set the tone by acting as role models for personnel. They must adopt a viable personal strategy for facilitating change in the workplace culture.

VII Managing a More Educated Workplace

More and more of today's sworn police personnel have more than two years of college education. College-educated officers tend to have greater strengths in many key areas than their non-college-educated counterparts; however, they also seem to experience more stress and are more likely to question orders, request more frequent reassignment, have lower morale and more absenteeism, and become frustrated more easily by bureaucratic procedures.

Supervisors need to empower their subordinates, and thus expand their own influence as leaders. This comes through delegation and allowing meaningful participation in decision-making. Empowerment leads to employees accepting responsibility for a job well done. Effective delegation leads to effective supervision, but effective delegation takes thought and preparation. The success or failure of empowerment depends on the commitment and human skills possessed by those seeking to implement it. Increased employee participation and effective delegation benefit the community, the police department, first-line supervisors, and employees.

Empowerment is essential in order to recruit and retain college-educated officers. Sergeants are the key to the empowerment process. They must believe that people are their greatest asset and reject the supervisor's traditional role as an overseer of "employees" in the workplace.

VIII *Training for the New Supervisor*

Even if sergeants are committed to fairness and equal opportunity employment, they need training to develop the necessary skills. They should be given on-the-job coaching and evaluation by a certified trainer. Unfortunately, budgetary problems mean that training needs are often abandoned. However, supervisory training is necessary to lower the percentage of vicarious liability cases and to reduce potentially disruptive behavior involving nontraditional employees. Proactive police managers know that the only way to guard against these potential problems is to strengthen the rank of sergeant through selective promotion, upgraded supervisory training, and unequivocal support.

Multiple-Choice Questions (Circle the Best Answer)

1. William H. Parker referred to the security of the "womb" of the police society as the

    a. shell of majoritism.

    b. shell of minoritism.

    c. thin blue line.

    d. security blanket.

2. The importance of attracting women and minority officers is

    a. providing them with government jobs to meet quotas.

    b. effective policing.

    c. that it is cost-effective.

    d. they work for less money.

3. Discrimination institutionalized by law is

   a. de facto.

   b. de jure.

   c. case law.

   d. stare decisis.

4. College-educated officers tend to experience _____ than their less-educated colleagues.

   a. more stress

   b. greater enthusiasm

   c. higher morale

   d. less absenteeism

5. According to Gary Johns, _____ is normal human behavior.

   a. prejudice

   b. prejudgment

   c. bigotry

   d. stereotype

6. Negative and unfavorable treatment of people based on their membership in a particular group is

   a. prejudice.

   b. stereotype.

   c. discrimination.

   d. xenophobia.

7. Group-shared negative attitudes based on tradition or ignorance that assign similar undesirable attributes to all members of the out group refer to

   a. prejudgment.

   b. stereotype.

   c. discrimination.

   d. ethnocentrism.

8. A negative attitude toward a particular group considered different and inferior is

    a. prejudice.

    b. stereotype.

    c. discrimination.

    d. bigotry.

9. Sexual harassment is prohibited by the

    a. Civil Rights Act.

    b. Quid Pro Quo Act.

    c. Protected Class Act.

    d. Equal Treatment under the Law Act.

10. The natural tendency of human beings to view their own culture and customs as right and superior and to judge all others by those standards is called

    a. prejudice.

    b. discrimination.

    c. ethnocentrism.

    d. xenophobia.

11. The irrational fear or hatred of strangers and foreigners is called

    a. ethnocentrism.

    b. discrimination.

    c. stereotype.

    d. xenophobia.

12. The Civil Rights Act of _____ prohibited discrimination based on national origin, ethnic group, creed, sex, race, or age.

    a. 1972

    b. 1965

    c. 1964

    d. 1966

13. Title _____ of the Civil Rights Act prohibited employers and unions from discriminating against employees.

    a. IV
    b. VI
    c. VII
    d. VIII

14. Which of the following was created under authority of Title VII as amended in 1966?

    a. Civil Rights Act.
    b. Guidelines on Employee Selection Procedures.
    c. Equal Employment Opportunity Commission.
    d. Affirmative Action.

15. Which of the following required employers to take positive steps to overcome present and past discrimination in order to achieve equal employment opportunity?

    a. Civil Rights Act.
    b. Guidelines on Employee Selection Procedures.
    c. EEOC.
    d. Affirmative Action.

16. Which guidelines adopted by the commission were designed to promote activism without creating reverse discrimination prohibited by the Civil Rights Act?

    a. Guidelines on Employee Selection Procedures.
    b. EEOC.
    c. Affirmative Action.
    d. Americans with Disabilities Act.

17. Which of the following stressed the need for "goals," "timetables," and "actions" designed to deal with discrimination?

    a. Guidelines on Employee Selection Procedures.
    b. Equal Employment Selection Procedures.

c. Affirmative Action.

d. Americans with Disabilities Act.

18. Which of the following involved the four basic steps that included continuous assessment of use patterns to prevent the reintroduction of discriminatory practices?

   a. Guidelines on Employee Selection Procedures.

   b. Equal Employment Selection Procedures.

   c. Affirmative Action.

   d. Civil Rights Act.

19. Which court case was used to force the Department of Public Safety of Alabama to hire one black trooper for each white trooper until 25 percent of all troopers were black?

   a. Brown v. Board of Education.

   b. Griggs v. Duke Power Company.

   c. NAACP v. Allen.

   d. NAACP v. Bakke.

20. The _____ decision protected police officers from arbitrary and discriminatory screening during testing procedures.

   a. Brown v. Board of Education

   b. Griggs v. Duke Power Company

   c. NAACP v. Allen

   d. NAACP v. Bakke

21. _____ is when individual employees are subjected to suggestive comments.

   a. Quid pro quo sexual harassment

   b. Hostile work environment sexual harassment

   c. Entrapment

   d. Verbal assault

22. For hostile work environment sexual harassment, all of the following are elements except the

   a. conduct is unwelcome.

   b. conduct is perceived by the victim as hostile or abusive.

   c. victim is forced to grant sexual favors to maintain employment status.

   d. conduct is sufficiently severe or pervasive so as to alter the conditions of the victim's employment and create an abusive work environment.

23. _____ substitutes self-supervision for traditional organizational control mechanisms.

   a. Authority

   b. Autonomy

   c. Empowerment

   d. Isolation

24. According to a Pew Research study, _____ percent of women who worked in male-dominated professions, such as police work, considered sexual harassment a problem.

   a. 48

   b. 50

   c. 62

   d. 72

True or False Questions

1. No-win situations are the heart of the empowerment process.

2. New police sergeants will need extensive supervisory training and on-the-job coaching to be able to cope with the human relations challenge of the 2000s.

3. A Police Executive Research Forum survey found that college-educated police officers have lower morale.

4. Apathy is the key to understanding and utilizing the talents of gay personnel.

5. If a supervisor actively participates in harassment of an employee, the police department and the governmental entity of which it is a part can be held liable.

6. Empathic supervisors can quickly subvert an otherwise effective anti-harassment policy.

7. Supportive and reactive supervisors are in a strategic position to assist other police managers in spotting and stopping sexual harassment.

8. Under Title VII of the Civil Rights Act, sexual harassment between co-workers produces employer liability and is considered an action of the employer.

9. Brown v. Board of Education, Kennedy's Camelot, and the Johnson administration's desire to create a discrimination-free society fostered the desire to create what was called "a perfect society."

10. According to the federal government's policy on Affirmative Action, an employer is never required to hire a person who does not have the qualifications needed to perform the job successfully.

11. Validity is consistency with which any test yields accurate measurements.

12. Reliability simply means that the test measures what it is supposed to measure.

13. White male sergeants must understand that many of their nontraditional employees have been conditioned to expect the worst.

14. Favoritism and privilege are absolutely essential in effective supervision.

15. Effective supervision always begins with an awareness of the individual and cultural differences among employees.

16. To do the job right, supervisors need technical, human, administrative, and problem-solving skills.

CHAPTER 14 Tactical Operations—Critical Incident Deployment

LEARNING OBJECTIVES

1. Describe what a critical incident deployment is.
2. Describe the categories of a critical incident deployment.
3. List information that can be obtained for precritical incident deployments.
4. Understand the relationship between an Incident Command System and a critical incident deployment.
5. Understand the role of the first-line supervisor and a critical incident deployment.
6. Describe the critical incident debriefing and its importance.

KEY TERMS

- critical incident
- critical incident stress management
- emotional debriefing
- federal emergency
- Incident Command System
- management agency
- post-traumatic stress disorder
- special weapons and tactics
- strike team
- tactical debriefing
- tactical operation
- task force

Chapter Summary

A **critical incident** is any event or situation that causes or has the potential to cause harm, serious bodily injury or death, property damage, legal involvement, and media activity. Such situations may range from relatively low-scale local operations, such as locating missing children, dignitary protection (including high-profile arrested suspects), domestic hostage taking and traffic incidents, to multijurisdictional major deployment of emergency personnel, such as terrorist attacks and weather-related catastrophes. The US Department of Homeland Security has recommended that all police agencies use the **Incident Command System** (ICS) model for responding to any critical incident, regardless of the size and scope. The ICS model is flexible enough to be used in a wide variety of critical incident responses and allows for the use of common terminology, effective inter- and intra-agency communications, and accountability. One important feature of critical incident management is the debriefing process. Debriefing allows for mistakes to be identified and corrected for future critical incident deployments, and to identify and treat stress problems that may surface with emergency responders. One area of critical incident deployment that receives the most media attention is the use of Special Weapons and Tactics (SWAT) or tactical teams. The National Tactical Officers Association has established guidelines for local law enforcement agencies to use when considering creation of a tactical team. These guidelines point to the need for proper planning, written policies and procedures, and the judicial use of force in critical incident responses.

Multiple-Choice Questions (Circle the Best Answer)

1. A type of call received by police and sheriff's departments that normally would not require rapid deployment of officers, equipment, and other emergency personnel is

    a. theft of property.

    b. safety and rescue.

    c. criminal or threat incidents.

    d. man-made or severe disasters.

2. Boltz and Solis suggest the need for police and sheriff's departments to collect information that may be useful during critical incidents. This is called

    a. precrisis intelligence.

    b. predisaster information.

    c. preincident intelligence.

    d. preincident information.

3. The system designed to provide a consistent nationwide approach for federal, state, and local governments to work effectively and efficiently together during incidents is

   a. National Incident Management System (NIMS).
   b. ICS.
   c. Federal Emergency Management Agency (FEMA).
   d. SWAT.

4. The three basic elements of the ICS are

   a. local terminology, interaction, and accountability.
   b. common terminology, communications, and resources.
   c. accountability, common terminology, and communications.
   d. communications, common frequencies, and local terminology.

5. The two main priorities for a first-line supervisor on the scene of a critical incident are

   a. communicate and record.
   b. act and control.
   c. record and act.
   d. act and communicate.

6. The five management functions of the ICS are

   a. incident command, operations, planning, logistics, finance/administration.
   b. planning, incident reporting, operations, finance/administration, logistics.
   c. incident reporting, planning, finance/administration, logistics, operations.
   d. incident command, operations, planning, finance, administration.

7. The person who serves as a conduit of information to the media during critical incidents is the

   a. safety officer.
   b. liaison officer.

c. public information officer.

d. communications officer.

8. While the span of control may vary, FEMA recommends a ratio of

   a. one supervisor to seven reporting officers.

   b. one supervisor to six reporting officers.

   c. one supervisor to five reporting officers.

   d. one supervisor to four reporting officers.

9. If additional supervisory levels are needed beyond the recommended FEMA ratio, FEMA recommends adding the following levels to the operations function:

   a. divisions, groups, sections.

   b. sections, divisions, departments.

   c. division, branches, groups.

   d. branches, divisions, sections.

10. The two major purposes of debriefings are

    a. tactical and emotional.

    b. information and accountability.

    c. results and information.

    d. information and understanding.

11. According to Evans and Coman, two of the more frequently reported reasons for police officer resignations are

    a. stress and departmental policies/procedures.

    b. departmental policies/procedures and quality of supervision.

    c. supervision and stress.

    d. stress and overwork.

True or False Questions

1. Fires, both structural and woodland, would be an example of a man-made or natural disaster.

2. The need for precrisis intelligence is no longer considered a requirement.

3. The acronym CALEA stands for Commission on Accreditation for Law Enforcement Agencies.

4. The NIMS is designed to provide a consistent local approach for surrounding police and sheriff's departments to work together.

5. The acronym ICS stands for Incident Command System.

6. One of the basic elements of the ICS is unique terminology.

7. The first-line supervisor on the scene of a critical incident has two main priorities: to act and to communicate.

8. The officer who serves as the primary contact for supporting agencies assisting at an incident is the public information officer.

9. The recommended span of control by FEMA is one supervisor to five reporting officers.

10. The two types of debriefings are tactical and informative.

11. Militarization of the police has the potential to break ties within the community between citizens and law enforcement.

CHAPTER 15 Labor Relations—Problem Solving through Constructive Conflict

LEARNING OBJECTIVES

1. Explore the hidden revolution in police labor relations.
2. Define collective bargaining and outline the steps involved in choosing a bargaining agent.
3. Describe constructive conflict and understand its relationship to participatory management.
4. Recognize management rights.
5. Understand the need for a strong management rights clause.
6. Identify goals that unions seek to achieve through bargaining.
7. Compare and contrast the methods used to resolve impasses in contract negotiations.
8. Define a job action and describe those that have been used in police work.
9. Define the word contract based on its meaning in labor law.
10. Contrast collective bargaining with contract administration.
11. Identify the sergeant's unique role in labor relations and contract administration.
12. Appreciate the need for and value of a dynamic balance between labor and management.
13. Recognize the subtle shift from the traditional to an interest-based collective bargaining process.

KEY TERMS

- balance through constructive conflict
- bargaining in good faith
- choosing a bargaining agent
- collective bargaining
- designated rights
- exclusive bargaining agent
- grievance
- impasse resolution techniques
- management rights/union responsibility
- negotiating a CBA or contract
- noneconomic issues
- participatory management by contracts
- reserved rights
- role conflict and its impact on morale
- scope of bargaining
- sergeants as contract administrators
- "traditional" versus "innovative" bargaining
- sergeants as disciplinarians
- union security measures
- unionism—the hidden revolution
- wages, hours, and conditions of employment

Chapter Summary

Labor unions were banned in the United States until the mid-1930s, with the passing of the Wagner Act, known as the National Labor Relations Act. However, government employees were specifically denied the right to **collective bargaining**, and they became increasingly militant in their demands for equal treatment in labor relations. The Boston police strike of 1919 was a landmark event that exposed the nation to governmental labor problems. The strike failed to meet its objectives, but it made officials sit up and take notice, toughening their stance against the collective bargaining process for public employees.

By the early 1940s, an informal collective bargaining process had developed with limited success, but it was likewise crushed by legislation, court decisions, police officials, and politicians. Government employees soon formed union-like professional associations that lobbied for legislative changes. By 1959, some limited rights to bargain were granted to public employees regarding wages, hours, and working conditions. The Public Employee Relations Act 195, passed in the late 1960s, became the prototype for collective bargaining statutes throughout the United States by permitting strikes by public employees in nonsafety categories.

Today, approximately 75 percent of all American police officers are due-paying members of labor unions. Many of these unions have developed from social or fraternal organizations. No national labor organization represents the interests of all police personnel, but national labor organizations do have political power.

Unionism and collective bargaining by police officers have been referred to as the "hidden revolution." Collective bargaining has become a vehicle for problem solving through constructive conflict. Balanced power between the union and management is the key to successful collective bargaining.

I *Management Rights*

Management rights refer to decisions governing the **conditions of employment** over which management claims to have exclusive jurisdiction.

1. **Reserved rights concept.** Presumes that management authority is supreme in all matters, except what is expressly conceded in the collective bargaining agreement or where authority is restricted by law. Thus, little or nothing is said about management rights in the **contract**.

2. **Designated rights concept.** Intended to clarify and reinforce the rights claimed by management. A management rights clause is part of the bargaining agreement to reduce confusion and misunderstanding.

II Understanding Bargaining

Collective bargaining is hailed as being good for organizational growth and development. It is built on the premise that controlled conflict between management and labor is good and necessary.

A. **Collective Bargaining.** The process by which a labor contract is negotiated and enforced between the employees' exclusive bargaining agent (union) and the state or local government operating the department. There is an affirmative duty to bargain, but neither side is obligated to accept a proposal or make a concession.

One of the first steps is for each side to select a negotiating team. The knowledge, skills, and dedication of the negotiators determine the quality of the agreement and set the tone for future labor relations.

Because police officers are not covered by the federal National Labor Relations Act of 1935, state legislation usually authorizes collective bargaining, meaning that most states have a State Labor Relations Board (SLRB) to administer the law and regulate the process. Once the SLRB accepts a petition for selection of a bargaining unit, it determines the composition of the unit, usually looking for a commonality of interests. While unions should represent employees whose jobs are similar and who share common interests, unfortunately, there has been little consistency in this regard. A formal hearing and election lead to selection of the bargaining unit, and the SLRB must certify the results. Certification of representation attests to the fact that a majority of those in the bargaining unit voted for the union. Certification of election results attests to the fact that the employees in the bargaining unit voted against union representation.

A certified police union is the exclusive bargaining agent for all members of the bargaining unit, whether they belong to the union or not. Management cannot negotiate directly with anyone other than the exclusive bargaining agent. Most states prohibit unfair labor practices and strive to keep labor and management coequal in the collective bargaining process.

Once the bargaining teams are formed, they must reach a consensus on the scope of the bargaining—the issues to be discussed. Normally, it is in management's interest to limit the scope of collective bargaining, whereas organized labor wants everything placed on the table for discussion.

Three types of bargaining proposals are outlined by the authors:

1. *Mandatory subjects.* These subjects, such as disability pay, occupational safety, and minimum staffing requirements, clearly fall within the category of wages, hours, and other terms and conditions of employment.

2. *Voluntary subjects.* These subjects, such as health club memberships, volume discounts on group purchases, and new benefits for retirees,

clearly fall outside the mandatory category, but are brought to the table for voluntary consideration. The other party is not required to bargain on them or include them in the contract.

3. *Illegal subjects.* These subjects, such as union shop agreements, binding arbitration, and the right to strike, have been specifically prohibited by the public employee bargaining law.

Rights and responsibility clauses are an integral component of the collective bargaining agreement. They are designed to limit the scope of the bargaining and delineate the areas of mutual concern. The power that management retains is spelled out in a management rights clause. A strong management rights clause gives management a great deal of control over operation of the department. This, along with a mutually acceptable no-strike impasse resolution process, is an essential part of an effective management strategy. Management rights clauses are usually negotiated along with an employee responsibility clause. Management rights and union responsibilities are the starting point for all future negotiations.

The basic purpose of bargaining is to reach a mutually acceptable agreement on the issues raised.

Proposals are generally classified into four categories: (1) nonnegotiable, (2) negotiable, (3) trade-off, or (4) expendable.

Once a particular issue is raised, the other team is obligated to respond in one of the four ways: (1) accepted, (2) accepted with minor modification, (3) rejected, or (4) rejected with counterproposal. In order to bargain in good faith, an opponent cannot reject an issue, clause, or proposal without an explanation.

III   Union Goals

A union's goals usually fall into seven categories:

1. Wages and working conditions.

2. Union security measures.

3. Impasse resolution techniques.

4. Meet-and-discuss provisions.

5. Grievance procedures.

6. Procedural due process.

7. Job security and seniority.

Two additional areas that have surfaced in recent years are as follows:

1. Officer safety regarding personnel deployment, workplace security, and equipment.
2. Adequate insurance coverage and the maintenance of fully paid health care benefits for officers who have been injured on or retire from the job.

Union bargaining teams also place great importance on negotiating strong security measures in the form of dues checkoff, maintenance of membership, and compulsory participation. However, many states with "right-to-work" statutes outlaw most union security measures.

Impasse resolution techniques are used to prevent police strikes. The most common being used in law enforcement bargaining are as follows:

1. Mediation.
2. Fact-finding.
3. Final best offer arbitration.
4. Binding arbitration.

Binding arbitration is the most popular method; its power to work is found in the collective bargaining agreement, state law, local ordinances, jurisdictional policy, and court decisions.

Communication is key to the collective bargaining process and successful conflict management. Meet-and-discuss sessions are the vehicle for participatory management.

IV Grievances

A. Grievance. Complaint arising out of the interpretation, application, or compliance with provisions of a collective bargaining agreement. Grievance procedures and due process are built into virtually every labor contract. Procedural due process is considered a must by all union members.

V Impasse Resolution through Job Actions

Most police union goals are achieved at the bargaining table or through skilful political manipulation. When this fails, the union may resort to coercive strategy. While union leaders tend to oppose the tactical use of job actions, they know that job actions are often a necessary part of the process. A job action should always be the impasse resolution of last resort.

A. Job Action. Calculated disruption in normally assigned duties. The purpose of job actions is to give the message that the collective bargaining process has broken down and that conflict is becoming unhealthy and disruptive. There are four basic types of job actions:

1. No-confidence votes.
2. Work slowdowns.
3. Work speedups.
4. Work stoppage.

While job actions may achieve the union's objectives, they create fear, anxiety, resentment, and a sense of betrayal in the community. The community will remember this fear long after the negotiation's issues or problems are over.

VI Contract Administration

Signing a contract guarantees continuation of the collective bargaining relationship for the duration of the agreement. An important part of contract administration is dissemination of information to all members concerning anything affected by the new agreement. A police labor contract is a living document. The parties must work hard to interpret language, work out bugs, make adjustments, resolve problems through a formal grievance process, and reach ethical compromises that serve the interests of employees, department, and community.

VII Role of the Sergeant in Collective Bargaining

Sergeants are in a difficult position between management and labor. The sergeant holds the key to the success of the contract. It is also the sergeant who must translate the labor policies into practice. The sergeant has the dual responsibility of helping subordinates and informing upper management of potential problems. The supervisor is the first to receive and resolve the grievances before they go to the command level. Inadequate supervisors feed the need for unions and cause labor relations to deteriorate.

First-line supervisors must understand labor relations and the positive aspect of constructive conflict. First-line supervisors facilitate communication, get cooperation, and coordinate day-to-day operations. Sergeants must realize that unresolved issues fester and destroy the purpose of policing. Considering the extensive job responsibilities that involve sergeants in planning, leading, controlling, and coaching of subordinates, it is clear that they are a part of management.

VIII Interest-Based Bargaining

A subtle shift appears to be under way, moving from traditional, position-based negotiations to innovative, win–win negotiations. Interest-based bargaining reduces confrontation and focuses on mutual interests, rather than preconceived positions. This bargaining method is gaining popularity and could revolutionize the way management approaches labor relations. These negotiation sessions have two criteria:

1. Dynamic interaction among team members unencumbered by formal environmental arrangements or occupational status considerations.
2. Open and candid discussion of mutual interests or concerns with respect to a particular issue.

Multiple-Choice Questions (Circle the Best Answer)

1. Which act, signed into law by President Franklin D. Roosevelt, was officially known as the National Labor Relations Act?

    a. Bosworth Act.

    b. Baker Act.

    c Myers Act.

    d. Wagner Act.

2. In 1945, union membership for blue-collar industries reached an all-time high of _____ percent of the workforce.

    a. 16.1

    b. 22.8

    c. 35.5

    d. 40.3

3. According to the World Almanac, it is now estimated that _____ percent of American workers are represented by unions.

    a. 10.3

    b. 22.8

    c. 35.5

    d. 40.3

4. Public employees at all levels of government resented that they were systematically excluded from collective bargaining and considered it to be an unwarranted intrusion on their _____ Amendment right to freedom of association.

   a. First
   b. Third
   c. Fifth
   d. Tenth

5. The Boston police strike of _____ is viewed by many unionists as one of the most important events in police history, giving the nation its first real exposure to labor problems in municipal government.

   a. 1945
   b. 1933
   c. 1919
   d. 1965

6. In 1959, _____ became the first state to grant public employees a limited right to bargain with their employer for wages, hours, and working conditions.

   a. Alaska
   b. Alabama
   c. Massachusetts
   d. Wisconsin

7. At the present time, more than _____ percent of the states have adopted legislation that permits public employees to participate in collective bargaining.

   a. 60
   b. 70
   c. 80
   d. 90

8. According to Cole and Smith, nearly _____ percent of all American police officers are due-paying members of labor unions today.

   a. 25

   b. 50

   c. 65

   d. 75

9. Unionism and collective bargaining are referred to by Samuel Walker as

   a. sowing the seeds of change.

   b. the hidden revolution.

   c. the wave of the future.

   d. the scope of bargaining.

10. Collective bargaining is a vehicle for problem solving through

    a. the decision-making process.

    b. unilateral decision-making.

    c. constructive conflict.

    d. vigorous debate.

11. Of the three types of bargaining proposals, which deals with new benefits for retirees?

    a. Mandatory subjects.

    b. Voluntary subjects.

    c. Illegal subjects.

    d. None of the above.

12. Of the three types of bargaining proposals, which deals with binding arbitration?

    a. Mandatory subjects.

    b. Voluntary subjects.

    c. Illegal subjects.

    d. None of the above.

13. Of the three types of bargaining proposals, which deals with disability?

    a. Mandatory subjects.

    b. Voluntary subjects.

    c. Illegal subjects.

    d. None of the above.

14. There are four basic categories in negotiating proposals. Which of the following includes items the negotiating team is willing to give up?

    a. Trade-off.

    b. Expendable.

    c. Nonnegotiable.

    d. Negotiable.

15. There are four basic categories in negotiating proposals. Which of the following includes items the negotiating team would like to have, but on which it is willing to compromise?

    a. Trade-off.

    b. Expendable.

    c. Nonnegotiable.

    d. Negotiable.

16. There are four impasse resolution techniques. Which of the following requires each side to submit a "final" offer, of which one will be binding?

    a. Mediation.

    b. Fact-finding.

    c. Final best offer arbitration.

    d. Binding arbitration.

17. There are four impasse resolution techniques. Which of the following involves the process of quasi-judicial hearings?

    a. Mediation.

    b. Fact-finding.

c. Final best offer arbitration.

   d. Binding arbitration.

18. There are four basic types of job actions. Which of the following alters the normal pace of life and generates public demands for a return to the status quo?

   a. No-confidence votes.

   b. Work slowdowns.

   c. Work speedups.

   d. Work stoppages.

19. There are four basic types of job actions. Which is designed to create anxiety and disruption in the public, producing social stress and precipitating demands for acquiescence to the union?

   a. No-confidence votes.

   b. Work slowdowns.

   c. Work speedups.

   d. Work stoppages.

20. Successful police work requires

   a. communication, cooperation, and ideal conditions.

   b. communication, cooperation, and coordination.

   c. communication, cooperation, and consideration.

   d. communication, consideration, and ideal conditions.

True or False Questions

1. The Myers Act was signed into law by Franklin D. Roosevelt in 1935.

2. The New York police strike of 1919 was the cause célèbre that gave the nation its first real exposure to labor problems in municipal government.

3. The Pennsylvania Public Employee Act of 1947 required public employees to bargain collectively with their employers.

4. The Pennsylvania Public Employee Act of 1947 forbids any and all strikes by public employees.

5. The dramatic rise of membership in police unions can, in large measure, be attributed to an influx of younger police officers.

6. Police unions have been forced to focus on national concerns more than on local issues.

7. The Police Benevolent Association can legitimately claim to represent the interests of all police personnel in the United States.

8. Samuel Walker refers to unionism and collective bargaining as the "open revolution."

9. Collective bargaining is a vehicle for problem solving through constructive conflict.

10. One of the most important issues in labor relations relates to the scope of bargaining.

11. Balanced power is the key to success in collective bargaining.

12. An organization needs someone to take charge and give it a sense of direction.

13. The designated rights concept presumes that management's authority is supreme in all matters, except those that have been expressly conceded in the collective bargaining agreement or where its authority is restricted by law.

14. The reserved rights concept is specifically intended to clarify and reinforce the rights claimed by management.

15. Collective bargaining is built on the assumption that a certain amount of controlled conflict is healthy.

16. Sergeants need to have a fairly comprehensive understanding of human behavior, work, workers, unions, and the collective bargaining process in order to do their job properly.

17. The National Labor Relations Act of 1935 covers police officers as public employees.

18. Certification of election results attests to the fact that employees in the bargaining unit voted for the union.

19. The initial bargaining session is a prelude to participatory management in police work.

20. Because there is an affirmative duty to bargain, both sides are required to accept a proposal and make concessions.

21. Selectivity is a prerequisite for success.

22. A strong responsibility clause gives the police administration a great deal of control over the operation of the department.

23. A weak responsibility clause gives away too much power.

24. The basic purpose of bargaining is to reach a mutually acceptable agreement on the issues raised at the table.

25. The first session at the bargaining table almost always sets the tone for subsequent meetings.

26. Innovative negotiations are known as position-based negotiations.

27. In healthy police organizations, sergeants are assimilated into the management team.

28. The sergeant's role is limited to contract implementation and administration.

29. Adequate supervisory personnel react to crisis situations.

30. Interest-based negotiations will never represent the wave of the future.

CHAPTER 16 Homeland Security and Terrorism—A Changing Role

LEARNING OBJECTIVES

1. Define terrorism.
2. Discuss the history and motives of terrorism.
3. Describe the different domestic terrorist groups.
4. Describe the conception and responsibility of the Department of Homeland Security.
5. List the FBI's three categories of foreign terrorist threats.
6. Discuss the functions of local law enforcement in identifying potential terrorist targets.
7. Describe the role and responsibility of first-line supervisors when managing terrorist threats.
8. Identify the types of situations in which police officers may be vulnerable to terrorist attacks.

KEY TERMS

- affective skills
- conceptual skills
- human skills
- Hu-TACK
- integrity
- knowledge-based skills
- loyalty
- management expectations of the supervisor
- officer behavior
- participation
- performance
- positive attitude
- responding to management
- self-appraisal
- supervisory skill areas
- tactical skills
- transition

Chapter Summary

Terrorism is generally defined as "the unlawful use of force or violence against persons or property to intimidate or coerce a government, the civilian population, or any segment thereof in furtherance of political or social objectives" (US Department of Justice). While the term terrorism is fairly new, acts of terrorism date back as far as the conception of communities. Terrorism falls into two categories: domestic and foreign. **Domestic terrorism** is carried out by persons who are citizens of the country against whom their attacks are targeted. **Foreign terrorism** is carried out by citizens of another country who target other countries.

I Domestic Terrorism

Domestic terrorism is, by far, the most common form of terrorism in the United States. Since the 1960s, domestic terrorism has increased in technology, frequency, and diversity. Advances in weapons, communication, and transportation technology have made it easier for domestic terrorists to create havoc on great masses of the population. Some of the more well-known organized terrorist groups include the Ku Klux Klan, the Weathermen, the Jewish Defense League, the Symbionese Liberation Army, the Army of God, the Animal Liberation Front, the Black Liberation Army, and the Aryan Nation. Single-issue terrorist groups may include antiabortion activists, animal rights activists, and environmentalists.

Domestic terrorism received very little public attention until the Oklahoma City Murrah Federal Building bombing. And, while some security measures were taken as a result of the bombing, the interest in domestic terrorism died until the September 11, 2001 attacks. With domestic terrorist shootings in San Bernadino, Orlando, Dallas, and Baton Rouge, the American people now recognize domestic terrorism as a major problem in the United States. A Gallup poll taken in 2015, just days after the Paris attacks, noted there was a 12 percent increase of fear among Americans that a terrorist attack would occur on US soil

II Foreign Terrorism

Foreign terrorist attacks on the United States have generally been religious based. The two worst attacks on American soil were the World Trade Center bombing in 1993 and the September 11, 2001 attacks. The FBI divides foreign terrorist threats into three categories:

1. Foreign sponsors of international terrorism—countries that sponsor, support, and/or fund terrorist groups and extremists.

2. Formalized terrorist groups—terrorists groups that have an organized infrastructure, training facilities, and financial backing.

3. Loosely affiliated international radical extremists—these may be unorganized groups or individuals who take it upon themselves to make terrorist attacks.

Among these, loosely affiliated terrorist groups and individuals pose the greatest risk to the United States. This is due in part to the difficulty of law enforcement intelligence to identify these individuals.

III American Response to Terrorism

In response to the 9/11 attacks, George W. Bush established a cabinet-level department known as the **Department of Homeland Security** (DHS). The DHS is the largest cabinet-level department and is responsible for coordinating 22 previously separate agencies in order to protect the United States against terrorist attacks. More specifically, the DHS coordinates the efforts of federal, state, and local law enforcement and emergency response agencies to prevent and respond to terrorist and natural disaster incidents. To help address this enormous effort, the DHS established the **National Infrastructure Protection Plan** (NIPP), which consists of six steps:

1. Establish security goals or performance targets that constitute a protective posture.

2. Identify assets, systems, networks, and functions within and outside the United States which require a level of protection.

3. Assess risks in terms of a direct or indirect attack on particular assets and the probability that a target will be attacked.

4. Establish priorities in terms of risk and levels of current protection and mitigation systems.

5. Implement protective programs for high-priority assets, especially those that currently have low levels of protection.

6. Measure effectiveness in terms of progress toward hardening assets and preventing attacks (Department of Homeland Security, 2006, p. 30).

After the 9/11 attacks, the FBI began to focus more on the need to increase intelligence and analysis related to terrorism by creating the Office of Intelligence. It also established the Counterterrorism Watch, which analyzes potential threats and provides daily reports to the president and other national security policymakers.

IV Local Response to Terrorism

Local police are typically the first responders to a terrorist attack. A primary goal of the DHS and the FBI is to help train, equip, provide intelligence, and support local law enforcement in preventing and responding to terrorist attacks. After the 9/11 attacks, new roles for state and local law enforcement emerged, including:

1. Coordinating homeland security at state and local levels.

2. Collecting, analyzing, and sharing critical information and intelligence.

3. Protecting critical infrastructure and key assets.

4. Securing the nation's borders, airports, and seaports.

5. Collaborating with federal, state, and local law enforcement agencies on taskforces.

6. Preparing for new response equipment, tactics, systems, and training (US Department of Justice, 2005).

There has long been a tradition of turf wars between local and federal law enforcement. Local law enforcement is wary of sharing information with federal law enforcement in fear of having worked diligently, only to have a case, along with the credit, taken away. This is changing, however. The FBI has now become more selective in what criminal cases it becomes involved in, leaving state and local law enforcement a greater role in investigating and prosecuting financial crimes, bank robbery, drug trafficking, and organized crime (US Department of Justice, 2005).

V Information versus Intelligence

Misunderstanding between the definitions of information versus intelligence occasionally occurs. Pieces of information gathered from diverse sources are simply raw data that frequently have limited inherent meaning. Intelligence is when a wide array of raw information is assessed for validity, reliability, and materiality to the issues in question, and is subjected to inductive and deductive reasoning. More specifically, the Association of Chiefs of Police (2002) defines intelligence as "the combination of credible information with quality-analysis information that has been evaluated and from which conclusions have been drawn" (p. 5).

VI Identifying Potential Terrorist Targets

One of the major roles of local law enforcement is to identify potential targets of terrorist attacks. This involves identifying critical infrastructure assets (dams, shopping malls, medical facilities, schools, and mass transportation centers) and transient targets (sporting events, festivals, fairs, and carnivals). Once locations have been identified, surveillance can begin. This will help identify reconnaissance activity and hopefully prevent any attacks. The surveillance material should be reported to state and local fusion centers where the activity can be documented, shared, and analyzed.

VII Police Supervisor's Role

The first-line police supervisor has three primary responsibilities in dealing with a terrorist threat: safety, information, and effective first response. The first responsibility of the police supervisor is the safety of the public and subordinate officers. The supervisor should also be keenly aware of potential terrorist threats in seemingly routine police calls for service. Garrett (2002) notes that there are five types of situations in which police officers may be vulnerable to terrorist attacks:

1. *Routine traffic stops.* A police officer may unknowingly stop a radicalized terrorist for a moving violation or suspicious activity.
2. *Routine domestic disturbance and residence calls.* Officers may respond unknowingly to a terrorist's residence and find themselves faced with heavily armed and dangerous individuals.
3. *Public rallies and marches.* While the danger may not come from the organization holding an event, protestors and radicals may incite violence and attack officers present.
4. *Confrontations and standoffs.* These may be the result of any of the previously mentioned threats, but can also be a hostage situation.
5. *Revenge and retaliation.* A terrorist may target a police department headquarters, government offices, financial institutions, or individuals. In February 2010, Joseph Stack flew his single-engine plane into the Internal Revenue Service building in Austin, Texas. Stack's motivation for the attack was revenge and retaliation.

In the event of a terrorist attack, police and first-line supervisors are normally the first responders to the scene. Proper coordination is essential in response to any emergency situation. The Federal Emergency Management Agency has provided some training and guidelines for local law enforcement response to terrorist attacks. Also, the Office of Domestic Preparedness (US Department of Justice, 2002) has prepared guidelines for police, firefighters, emergency medical personnel, public works personnel, HazMat personnel, and emergency management personnel on first responder responsibilities.

Multiple-Choice Questions (Circle the Best Answer)

1. _____ terrorism is, by far, the most common form of terrorism.
   a. Foreign
   b. Domestic
   c. Organized
   d. Political

2. According to More and Miller, _____ terrorist groups may pose the most serious threat to the United States.

   a. foreign-sponsored
   b. formalized
   c. loosely affiliated
   d. cyber

3. President George W. Bush established the _____ as a cabinet-level department in response to the September 11, 2001 terrorist attacks.

   a. National Infrastructure Protection Plan
   b. Department of Homeland Security
   c. Terrorist Screening Center
   d. Suspicious Activity Reporting System

4. Agencies that moved from the Treasury Department to the Department of Homeland Security include all of the following except

   a. Customs.
   b. Secret Service.
   c. Federal Law Enforcement Training Center.
   d. The Federal Bureau of Investigation.

5. _____ is a global command center that constantly reviews and analyzes potential terrorist threats.

   a. Counterterrorism Watch
   b. Department of Homeland Security
   c. Terrorist Screening Operations Unit
   d. Information Sharing Environment

6. The _____ are normally the first responders to a terrorist attack.

   a. local police
   b. state police

c. FBI

   d. DHS

7. _____ is/are gathered from diverse sources that frequently have limited inherent meaning.

   a. Information

   b. Intelligence

   c. Cell phone data

   d. Internet search-engine data

8. Local state and law enforcement agencies have partnered with the FBI to form early warning teams called

   a. tactical teams.

   b. cells.

   c. fusion centers.

   d. intelligence centers.

9. _____ allows the adoption of consistent policies for sharing information between law enforcement agencies, while ensuring that privacy and civil liberties are protected.

   a. National Crime Information Center

   b. Terrorist Screening Operations Unit

   c. Suspicious Activity Reporting

   d. Nationwide SAR Initiative

10. The primary responsibilities of first-line supervisors in managing terrorist threats involve all of the following except

    a. effective first response.

    b. safety.

    c. verification.

    d. information.

11. In an effort to help protect officers against ambush and sniper attacks, most larger police departments began using

   a. two-officer patrols.

   b. Terrorist Screening Operations Unit.

   c. back-up officers.

   d. both a and c.

True or False Questions

1. Domestic terrorism accounted for 80 percent of the terrorist incidents prior to the 9/11 attacks.

2. During the 1960s, most domestic terrorism involved white racists, black militants, and anti-war activists.

3. Single-issue terrorist groups may include animal rights activists, anti-abortion activists, and environmentalists.

4. The Army of God terrorist group had a mission to overthrow the US government and change the policy of Vietnam.

5. According to More and Miller, foreign terrorist attacks on the United States are generally politically based.

6. According to the text, formalized terrorist groups may pose the greatest threat to the United States.

7. Different formalized terrorist organizations tend to stay divided in terms of beliefs and in the sharing of information.

8. The Department of Homeland Security is the largest cabinet-level department in the federal government.

9. A study conducted in Phoenix, Arizona, found that most residents were highly unlikely to report suspected terrorist activity.

10. Incident-level analysis is important as it can be analyzed at different levels of geographic locations.

11. A transient target includes any function that may attract large crowds of people on a temporary basis.

12. Police patrol officers and first-line supervisors are rarely the first to receive information regarding terrorist activities.

ANSWER KEY TO OBJECTIVE QUESTIONS

Chapter 1

Multiple-Choice Questions

1. c	8. a	15. d
2. d	9. a	16. c
3. b	10. b	17. b
4. d	11. d	18. b
5. b	12. e	19. d
6. d	13. b	20. c
7. c	14. a	

True or False Questions

1. T	6. F	11. T
2. F	7. F	12. T
3. T	8. T	13. T
4. T	9. F	14. T
5. T	10. T	15. F

Chapter 2

Multiple-Choice Questions

1. b	5. d	9. b
2. c	6. c	10. b
3. c	7. a	11. b
4. a	8. c	12. c

True or False Questions

1. F	7. F	13. F
2. T	8. T	14. F
3. T	9. T	15. T
4. T	10. F	16. F
5. F	11. T	17. T
6. F	12. T	

Chapter 3

Multiple-Choice Questions

1. b	10. b	19. b
2. b	11. b	20. c
3. a	12. c	21. a
4. b	13. a	22. b
5. a	14. a	23. a
6. a	15. d	24. b
7. b	16. a	25. d
8. b	17. a	26. c
9. a	18. d	27. c

True or False Questions

1. F
2. F
3. T
4. T
5. T
6. T
7. T
8. T
9. T
10. T
11. T
12. F
13. F
14. T
15. F
16. F

Chapter 4

Multiple-Choice Questions

1. d
2. d
3. b
4. a
5. c
6. c
7. b
8. d
9. c
10. a
11. b
12. d
13. b
14. a
15. a
16. d
17. a

True or False Questions

1. T
2. T
3. T
4. T
5. T
6. T
7. T
8. F
9. T
10. F
11. T
12. T
13. F
14. T
15. F
16. F
17. T
18. F
19. T

Chapter 5

Multiple-Choice Questions

1. c	6. a	11. b
2. c	7. d	12. d
3. a	8. c	13. c
4. b	9. c	14. a
5. c	10. c	15. d

True or False Questions

1. F	8. T	15. F
2. T	9. T	16. T
3. T	10. F	17. T
4. F	11. T	18. F
5. T	12. T	19. T
6. T	13. T	20. T
7. F	14. T	

Chapter 6

Multiple-Choice Questions

1. b	6. a	11. a
2. a	7. c	12. b
3. a	8. d	13. b
4. b	9. d	14. c
5. b	10. d	15. a

True or False Questions

1. F
2. F
3. F
4. T
5. T
6. T
7. T
8. T
9. T
10. F
11. F
12. T

Chapter 7

Multiple-Choice Questions

1. c
2. b
3. b
4. d
5. b
6. d
7. a

True or False Questions

1. T
2. T
3. T
4. T
5. F
6. F
7. T
8. T
9. T

Chapter 8

Multiple-Choice Questions

1. a
2. c
3. d
4. a
5. d
6. e
7. c
8. a
9. a
10. b
11. c
12. c

13. d	16. c	19. b
14. a	17. d	
15. c	18. a	

True or False Questions

1. T	5. T	9. T
2. T	6. F	10. F
3. T	7. F	11. F
4. T	8. F	12. T

Chapter 9

Multiple-Choice Questions

1. a	8. b	15. e
2. c	9. b	16. a
3. e	10. c	17. b
4. c	11. d	18. e
5. b	12. b	19. b
6. c	13. d	20. c
7. a	14. a	

True or False Questions

1. T	7. T	13. F
2. T	8. F	14. F
3. F	9. T	15. T
4. F	10. F	16. T
5. T	11. F	17. T
6. T	12. F	18. T

19. F	25. F	31. F
20. T	26. F	32. F
21. F	27. T	33. F
22. T	28. T	34. F
23. T	29. F	35. T
24. F	30. F	36. T

Chapter 10

Multiple-Choice Questions

1. d	6. d	11. b
2. b	7. c	12. d
3. c	8. b	13. b
4. d	9. c	
5. c	10. d	

True or False Questions

1. T	7. F	13. T
2. T	8. T	14. T
3. T	9. T	15. T
4. T	10. F	16. T
5. T	11. T	17. F
6. T	12. T	18. F

Chapter 11

Multiple-Choice Questions

1. d	3. a	5. b
2. d	4. a	6. b

7. a	13. b	19. c
8. d	14. b	20. b
9. b	15. a	21. d
10. c	16. b	22. b
11. c	17. d	
12. b	18. c	

True or False Questions

1. T	8. T	15. F
2. F	9. T	16. F
3. F	10. T	17. F
4. F	11. F	18. F
5. F	12. T	19. T
6. F	13. F	
7. T	14. T	

Chapter 12

Multiple-Choice Questions

1. b	8. c	15. a
2. d	9. a	16. d
3. b	10. c	17. b
4. c	11. c	18. d
5. c	12. b	
6. c	13. c	
7. d	14. c	

True or False Questions

1. F
2. T
3. T
4. T
5. F
6. F
7. F
8. F
9. T
10. F
11. F
12. F
13. T
14. F
15. T
16. T

Chapter 13

Multiple-Choice Questions

1. b
2. b
3. b
4. a
5. b
6. c
7. b
8. a
9. a
10. c
11. d
12. c
13. c
14. c
15. d
16. c
17. c
18. c
19. c
20. b
21. b
22. c
23. c
24. c

True or False Questions

1. F
2. T
3. T
4. F
5. T
6. F
7. F
8. F
9. F
10. T
11. F
12. F

13. T
14. F
15. T
16. T

Chapter 14

Multiple-Choice Questions

1. a
2. a
3. a
4. c
5. d
6. a
7. c
8. c
9. c
10. a
11. b

True or False Questions

1. T
2. F
3. T
4. F
5. T
6. F
7. T
8. F
9. T
10. F
11. T

Chapter 15

Multiple-Choice Questions

1. d
2. c
3. a
4. a
5. c
6. d
7. c
8. d
9. b
10. c
11. b
12. c
13. a
14. b
15. d
16. c
17. b
18. c
19. c
20. b

True or False Questions

1. F	11. T	21. T
2. F	12. T	22. F
3. F	13. F	23. F
4. T	14. F	24. T
5. T	15. T	25. T
6. F	16. T	26. F
7. F	17. F	27. T
8. F	18. F	28. T
9. T	19. T	29. F
10. T	20. F	30. F

Chapter 16

Multiple-Choice Questions

1. b	5. a	9. d
2. c	6. a	10. c
3. b	7. a	11. d
4. d	8. c	

True or False Questions

1. T	5. F	9. F
2. T	6. F	10. T
3. T	7. F	11. T
4. F	8. T	12. F

Printed in the USA
CPSIA information can be obtained
at www.ICGtesting.com
LVHW082133050524
779441LV00032B/999